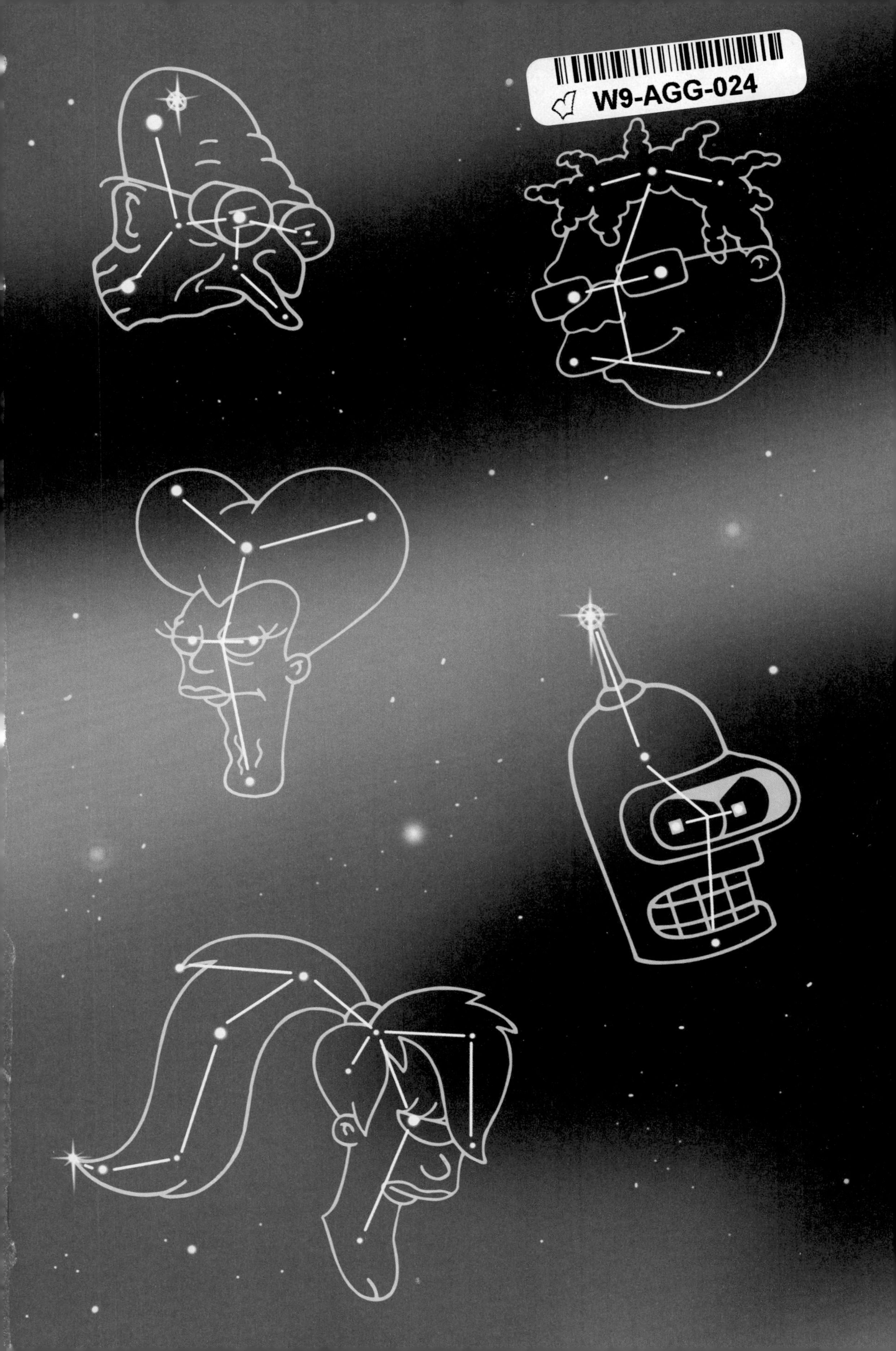

FUTURAMA™
CONQUERS THE UNIVERSE

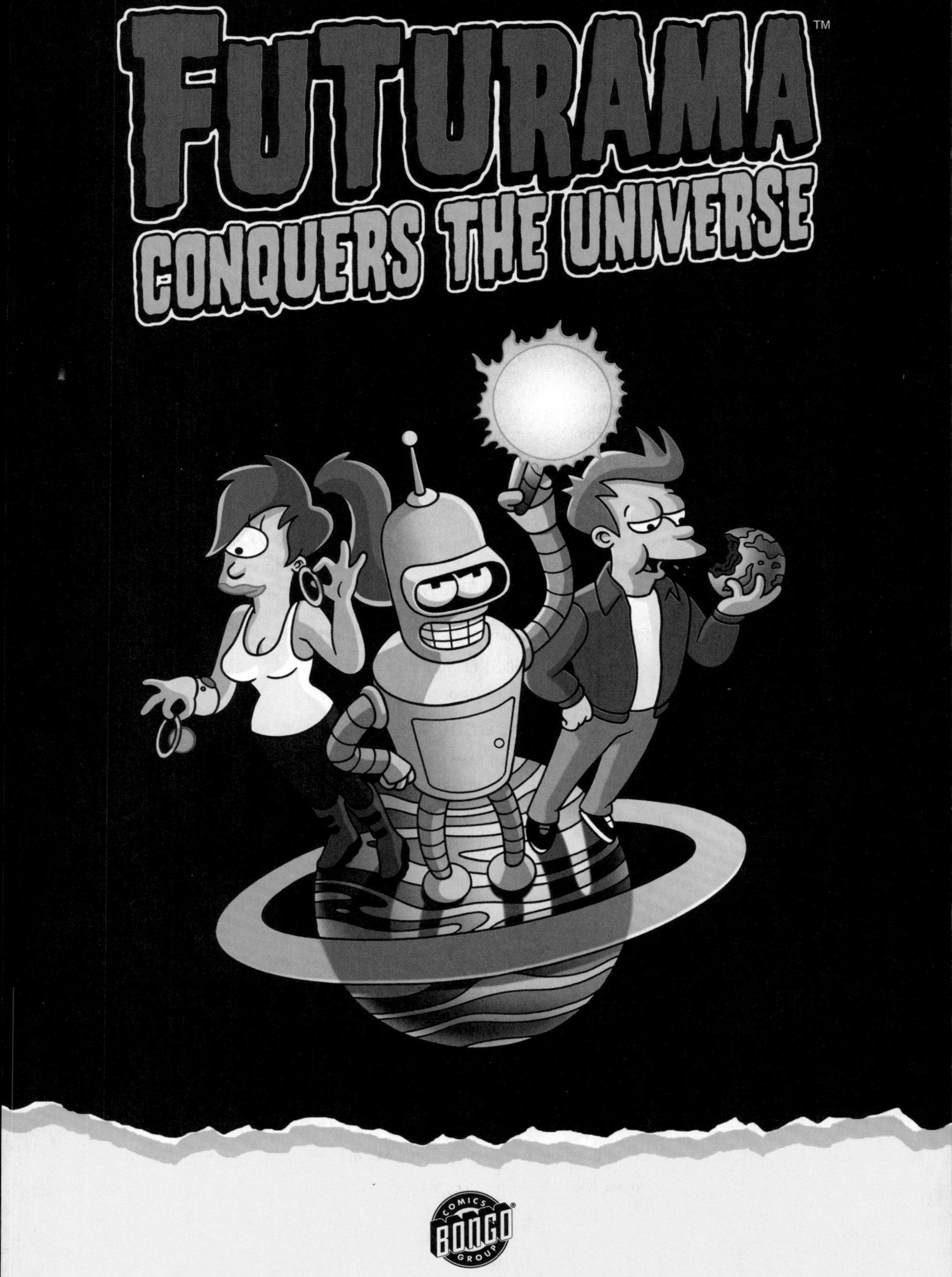

BONGO COMICS GROUP

FUTURAMA CONQUERS THE UNIVERSE

FIRST EDITION

ISBN: 978-1-892849-20-5

11 12 13 14 15 QG 10 9 8 7 6 5 4 3 2

Publisher: Matt Groening
Creative Director: Bill Morrison
Managing Editor: Terry Delegeane
Director of Operations: Robert Zaugh
Art Director: Nathan Kane
Art Director Special Projects: Serban Cristescu
Production Manager: Christopher Ungar
Legal Guardian: Susan A. Grode

Trade Paperback Concepts and Design: Serban Cristescu

HarperCollins Editors: Hope Innelli, Jeremy Cesarec

Contributing Artists:

Karen Bates, Serban Cristescu, Mike DeCarlo, John Delaney, Chia-Hsien Jason Ho,
Nathan Kane, Mike Kazaleh, Tom King, James Lloyd, Joey Mason, Bill Morrison, Phyllis Novin,
Andrew Pepoy, Mike Rote, Steve Steere Jr., Chris Ungar

Contributing Writers:
Ian Boothby, Eric Rogers, Patric M. Verrone

Printed by Quad/Graphics, Inc., Montreal, QC, Canada.
4/15/11

TABLE OF CONTENTS

07 .... THE BIG SWEEP

34 .... HOW TO DRAW FRY AND BENDER!

41 .... THE CURE FOR THE COMMON COLD

67 .... HOSTILE MAKEOVER

72 .... SIDESHOW FRY

100 .... THE BENDER YOU SAY

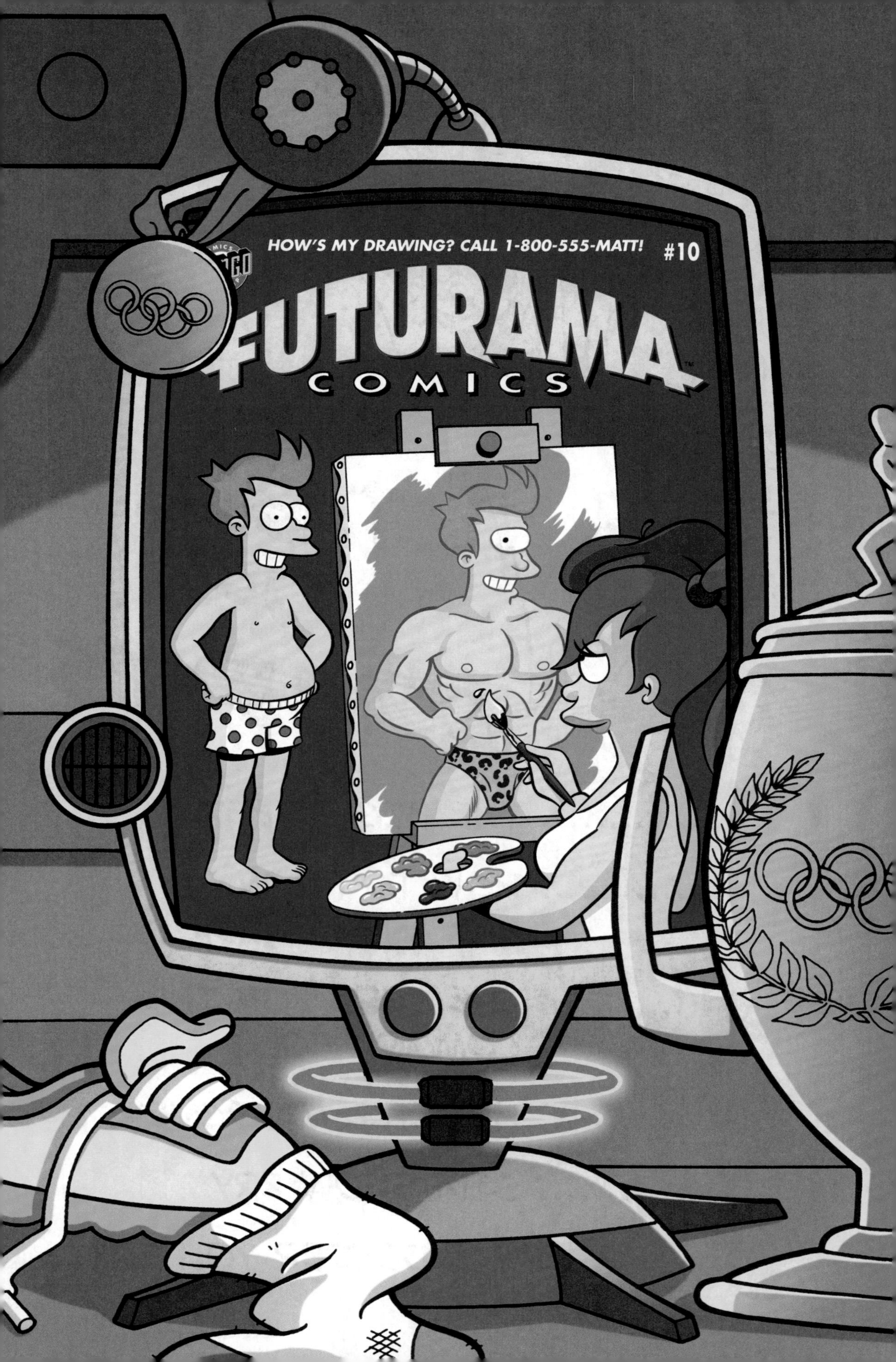
HOW'S MY DRAWING? CALL 1-800-555-MATT!
#10
FUTURAMA
COMICS

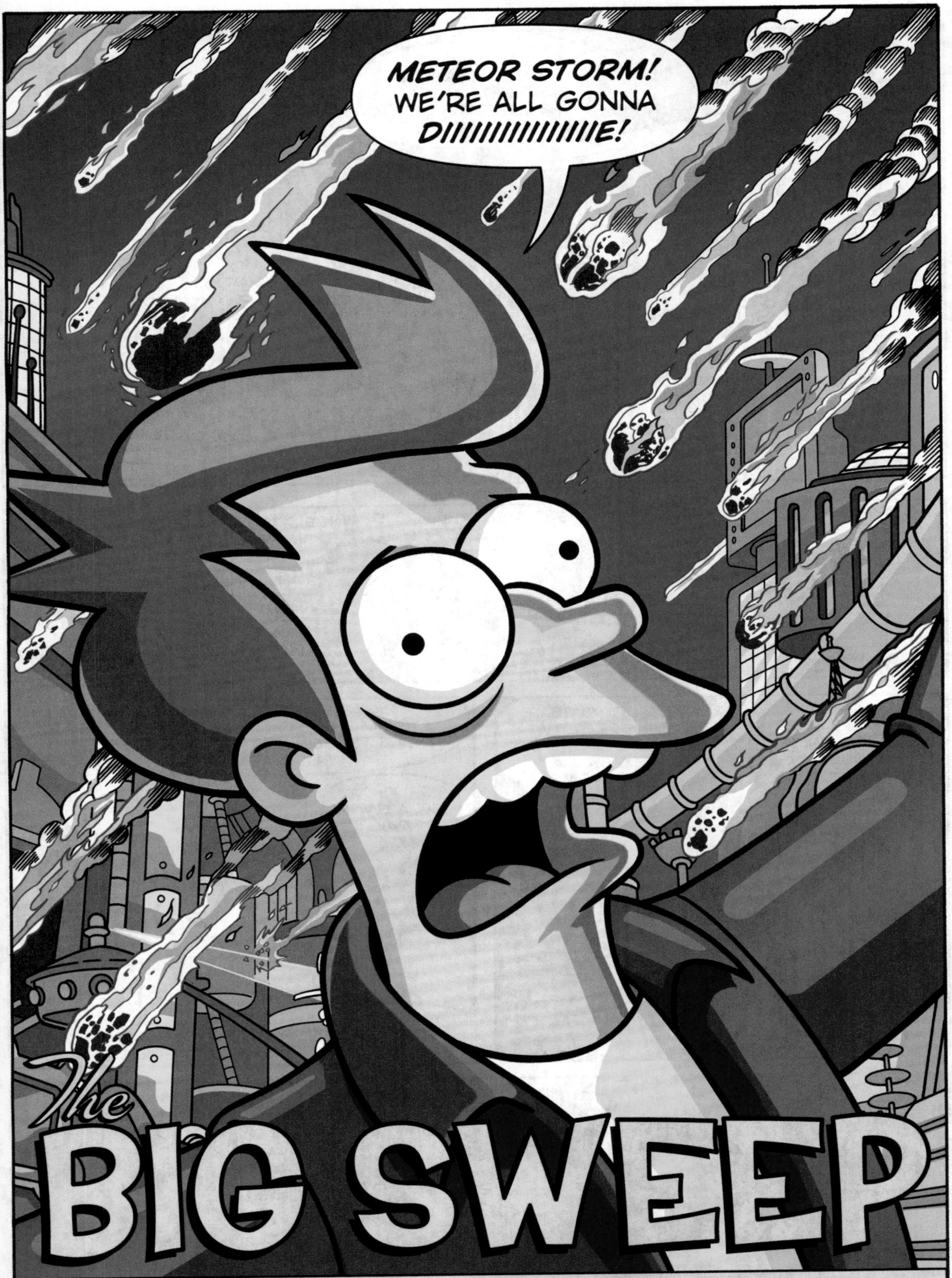
METEOR STORM! WE'RE ALL GONNA DIIIIIIIIIIIIIIIIE!
The BIG SWEEP

ERIC ROGERS script
JOHN DELANEY pencils
PHYLLIS NOVIN inks
JOEY MASON colors
KAREN BATES letters
BILL MORRISON editor
MATT GROENING ash commissioner

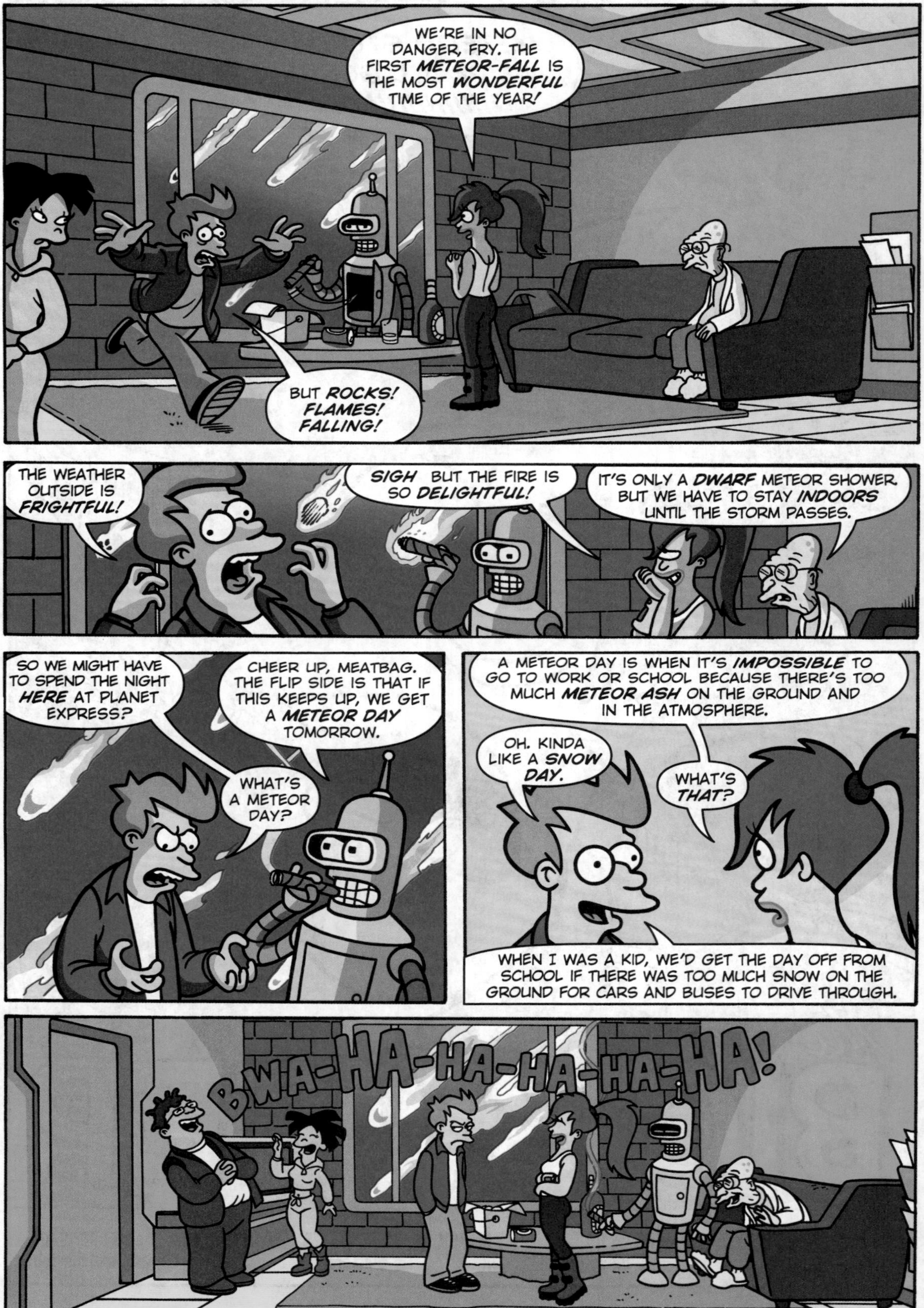
WE'RE IN NO DANGER, FRY. THE FIRST METEOR-FALL IS THE MOST WONDERFUL TIME OF THE YEAR!
BUT ROCKS! FLAMES! FALLING!
THE WEATHER OUTSIDE IS FRIGHTFUL!
SIGH BUT THE FIRE IS SO DELIGHTFUL!
IT'S ONLY A DWARF METEOR SHOWER, BUT WE HAVE TO STAY INDOORS UNTIL THE STORM PASSES.
SO WE MIGHT HAVE TO SPEND THE NIGHT HERE AT PLANET EXPRESS?
CHEER UP, MEATBAG. THE FLIP SIDE IS THAT IF THIS KEEPS UP, WE GET A METEOR DAY TOMORROW.
WHAT'S A METEOR DAY?
A METEOR DAY IS WHEN IT'S IMPOSSIBLE TO GO TO WORK OR SCHOOL BECAUSE THERE'S TOO MUCH METEOR ASH ON THE GROUND AND IN THE ATMOSPHERE.
OH. KINDA LIKE A SNOW DAY.
WHAT'S THAT?
WHEN I WAS A KID, WE'D GET THE DAY OFF FROM SCHOOL IF THERE WAS TOO MUCH SNOW ON THE GROUND FOR CARS AND BUSES TO DRIVE THROUGH.
BWA-HA-HA-HA-HA-HA!

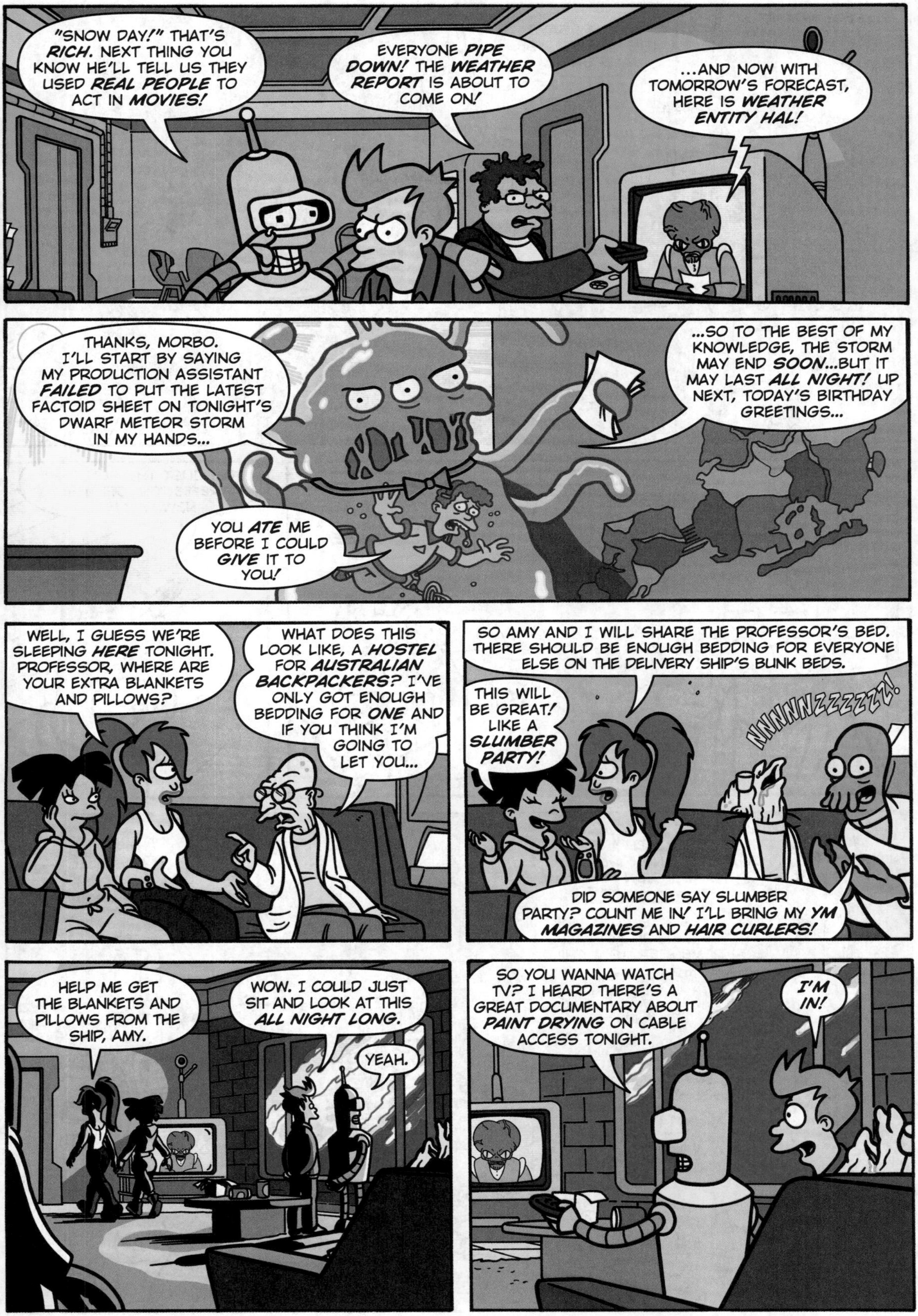
"SNOW DAY!" THAT'S RICH. NEXT THING YOU KNOW HE'LL TELL US THEY USED REAL PEOPLE TO ACT IN MOVIES!
EVERYONE PIPE DOWN! THE WEATHER REPORT IS ABOUT TO COME ON!
...AND NOW WITH TOMORROW'S FORECAST, HERE IS WEATHER ENTITY HAL!
THANKS, MORBO. I'LL START BY SAYING MY PRODUCTION ASSISTANT FAILED TO PUT THE LATEST FACTOID SHEET ON TONIGHT'S DWARF METEOR STORM IN MY HANDS...
YOU ATE ME BEFORE I COULD GIVE IT TO YOU!
...SO TO THE BEST OF MY KNOWLEDGE, THE STORM MAY END SOON...BUT IT MAY LAST ALL NIGHT! UP NEXT, TODAY'S BIRTHDAY GREETINGS...
WELL, I GUESS WE'RE SLEEPING HERE TONIGHT. PROFESSOR, WHERE ARE YOUR EXTRA BLANKETS AND PILLOWS?
WHAT DOES THIS LOOK LIKE, A HOSTEL FOR AUSTRALIAN BACKPACKERS? I'VE ONLY GOT ENOUGH BEDDING FOR ONE AND IF YOU THINK I'M GOING TO LET YOU...
SO AMY AND I WILL SHARE THE PROFESSOR'S BED. THERE SHOULD BE ENOUGH BEDDING FOR EVERYONE ELSE ON THE DELIVERY SHIP'S BUNK BEDS.
THIS WILL BE GREAT! LIKE A SLUMBER PARTY!
NNNNNZZZZZZ!
DID SOMEONE SAY SLUMBER PARTY? COUNT ME IN! I'LL BRING MY YM MAGAZINES AND HAIR CURLERS!
HELP ME GET THE BLANKETS AND PILLOWS FROM THE SHIP, AMY.
WOW. I COULD JUST SIT AND LOOK AT THIS ALL NIGHT LONG.
YEAH.
SO YOU WANNA WATCH TV? I HEARD THERE'S A GREAT DOCUMENTARY ABOUT PAINT DRYING ON CABLE ACCESS TONIGHT.
I'M IN!

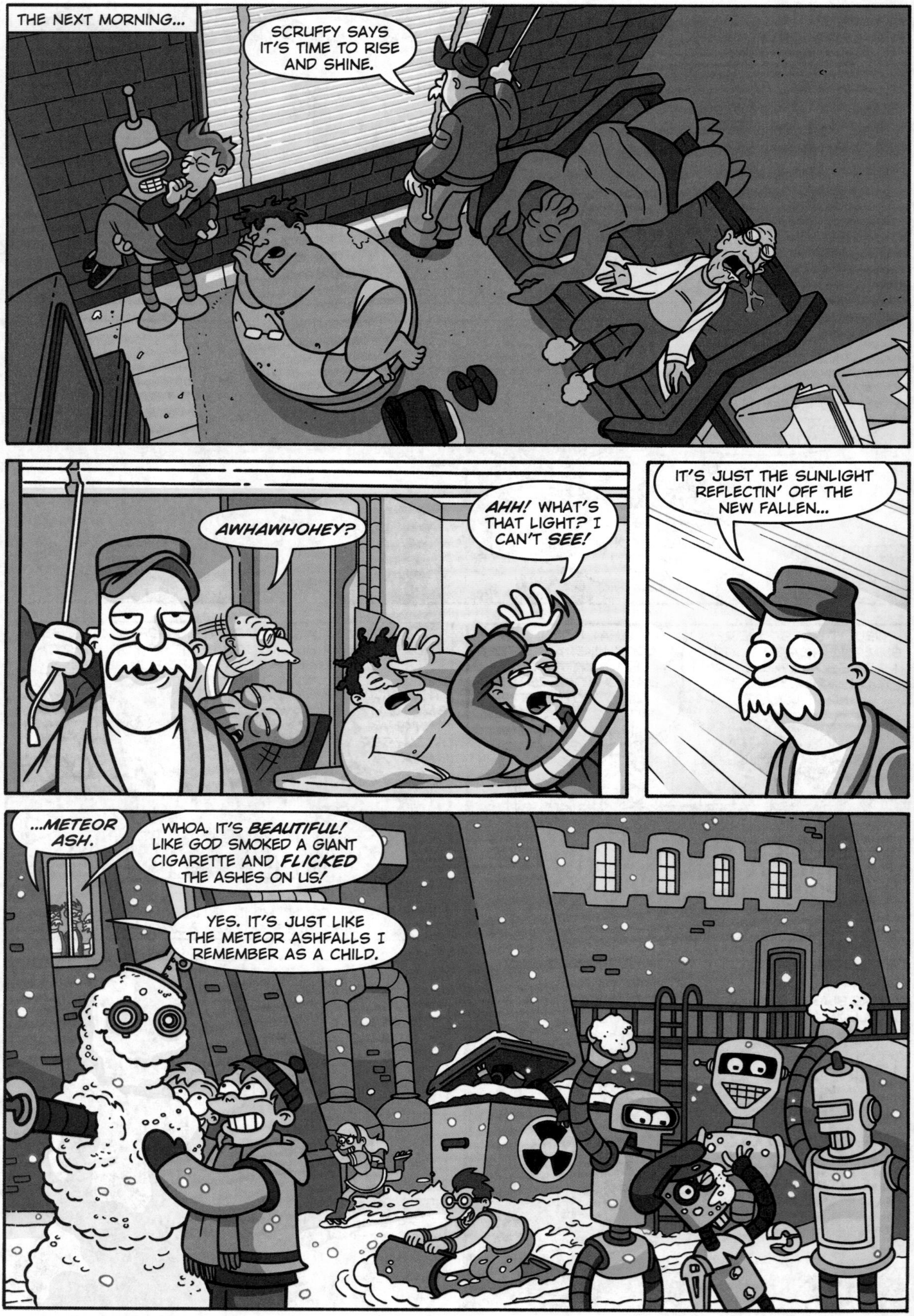
THE NEXT MORNING...
SCRUFFY SAYS IT'S TIME TO RISE AND SHINE.
AWHAWHOHEY?
AHH! WHAT'S THAT LIGHT? I CAN'T SEE!
IT'S JUST THE SUNLIGHT REFLECTIN' OFF THE NEW FALLEN...
...METEOR ASH.
WHOA. IT'S BEAUTIFUL! LIKE GOD SMOKED A GIANT CIGARETTE AND FLICKED THE ASHES ON US!
YES. IT'S JUST LIKE THE METEOR ASHFALLS I REMEMBER AS A CHILD.

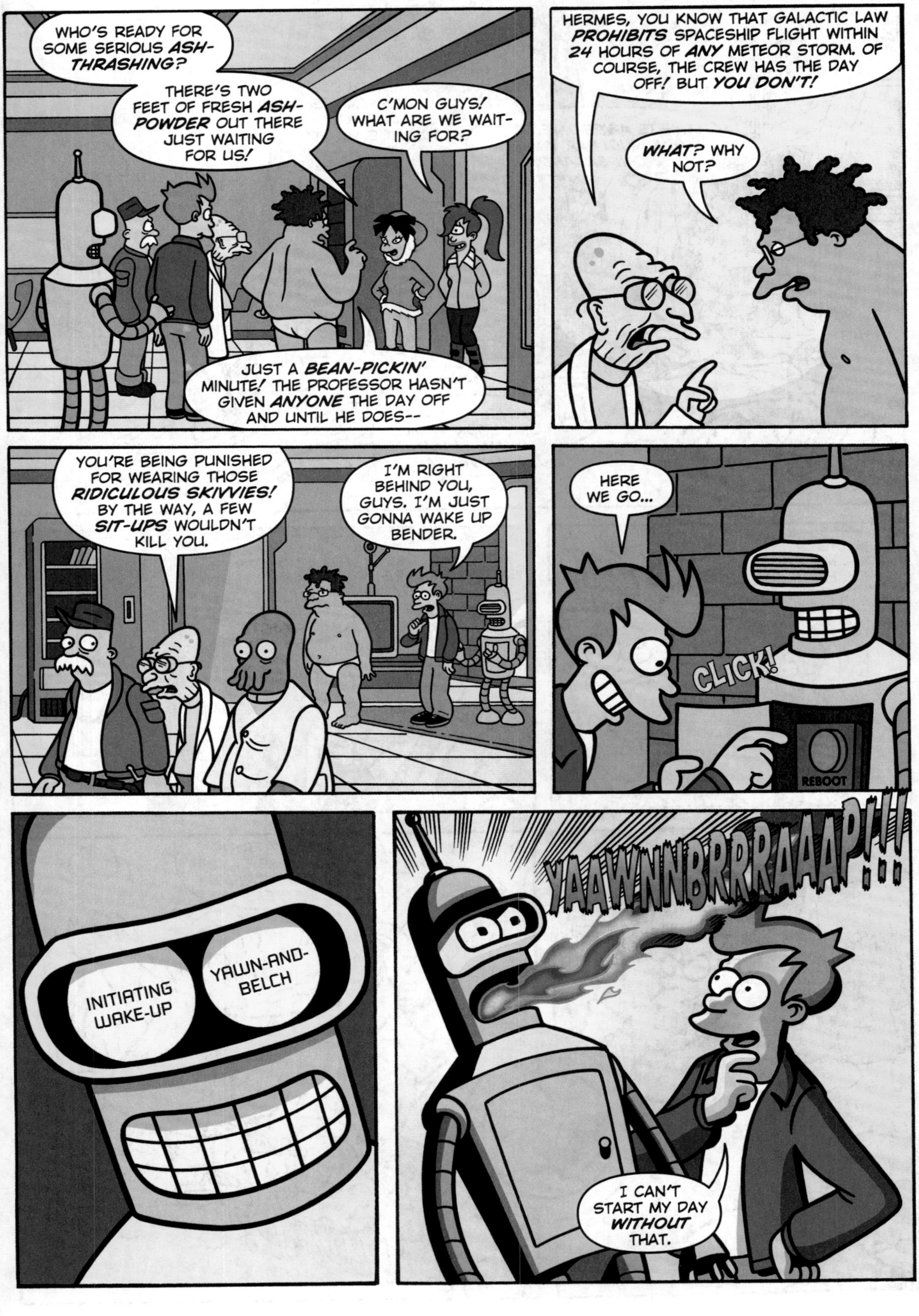
WHO'S READY FOR SOME SERIOUS ASH-THRASHING?
THERE'S TWO FEET OF FRESH ASH-POWDER OUT THERE JUST WAITING FOR US!
C'MON GUYS! WHAT ARE WE WAITING FOR?
JUST A BEAN-PICKIN' MINUTE! THE PROFESSOR HASN'T GIVEN ANYONE THE DAY OFF AND UNTIL HE DOES--
HERMES, YOU KNOW THAT GALACTIC LAW PROHIBITS SPACESHIP FLIGHT WITHIN 24 HOURS OF ANY METEOR STORM. OF COURSE, THE CREW HAS THE DAY OFF! BUT YOU DON'T!
WHAT? WHY NOT?
YOU'RE BEING PUNISHED FOR WEARING THOSE RIDICULOUS SKIVVIES! BY THE WAY, A FEW SIT-UPS WOULDN'T KILL YOU.
I'M RIGHT BEHIND YOU, GUYS. I'M JUST GONNA WAKE UP BENDER.
HERE WE GO...
CLICK!
REBOOT
INITIATING WAKE-UP
YAWN-AND-BELCH
YAAWNNBRRRAAAP!!!
I CAN'T START MY DAY WITHOUT THAT.

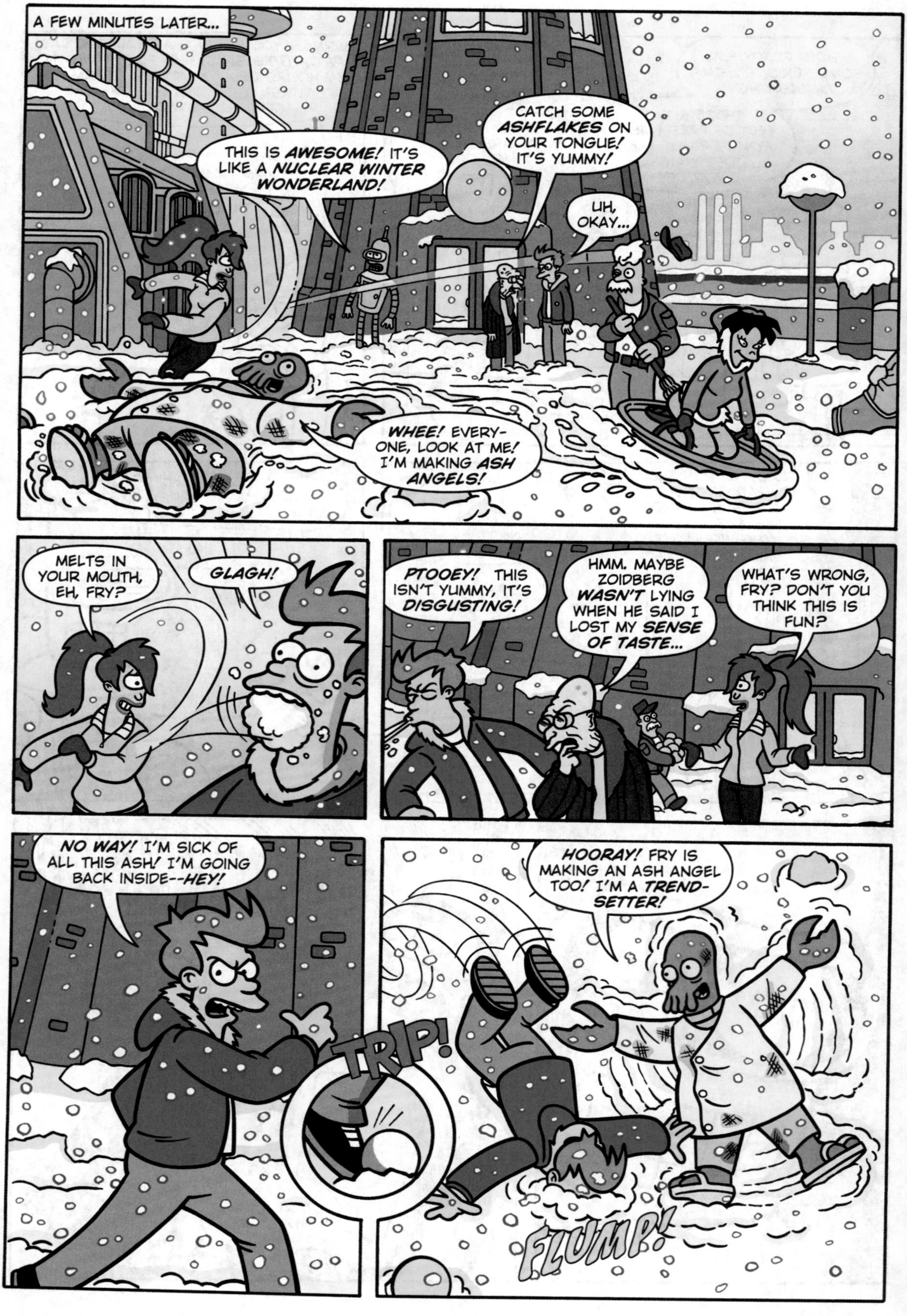
A FEW MINUTES LATER...
THIS IS AWESOME! IT'S LIKE A NUCLEAR WINTER WONDERLAND!
CATCH SOME ASHFLAKES ON YOUR TONGUE! IT'S YUMMY!
UH, OKAY...
WHEE! EVERY-ONE, LOOK AT ME! I'M MAKING ASH ANGELS!
MELTS IN YOUR MOUTH, EH, FRY?
GLAGH!
PTOOEY! THIS ISN'T YUMMY, IT'S DISGUSTING!
HMM. MAYBE ZOIDBERG WASN'T LYING WHEN HE SAID I LOST MY SENSE OF TASTE...
WHAT'S WRONG, FRY? DON'T YOU THINK THIS IS FUN?
NO WAY! I'M SICK OF ALL THIS ASH! I'M GOING BACK INSIDE--HEY!
TRIP!
HOORAY! FRY IS MAKING AN ASH ANGEL TOO! I'M A TREND-SETTER!
FLUMP!

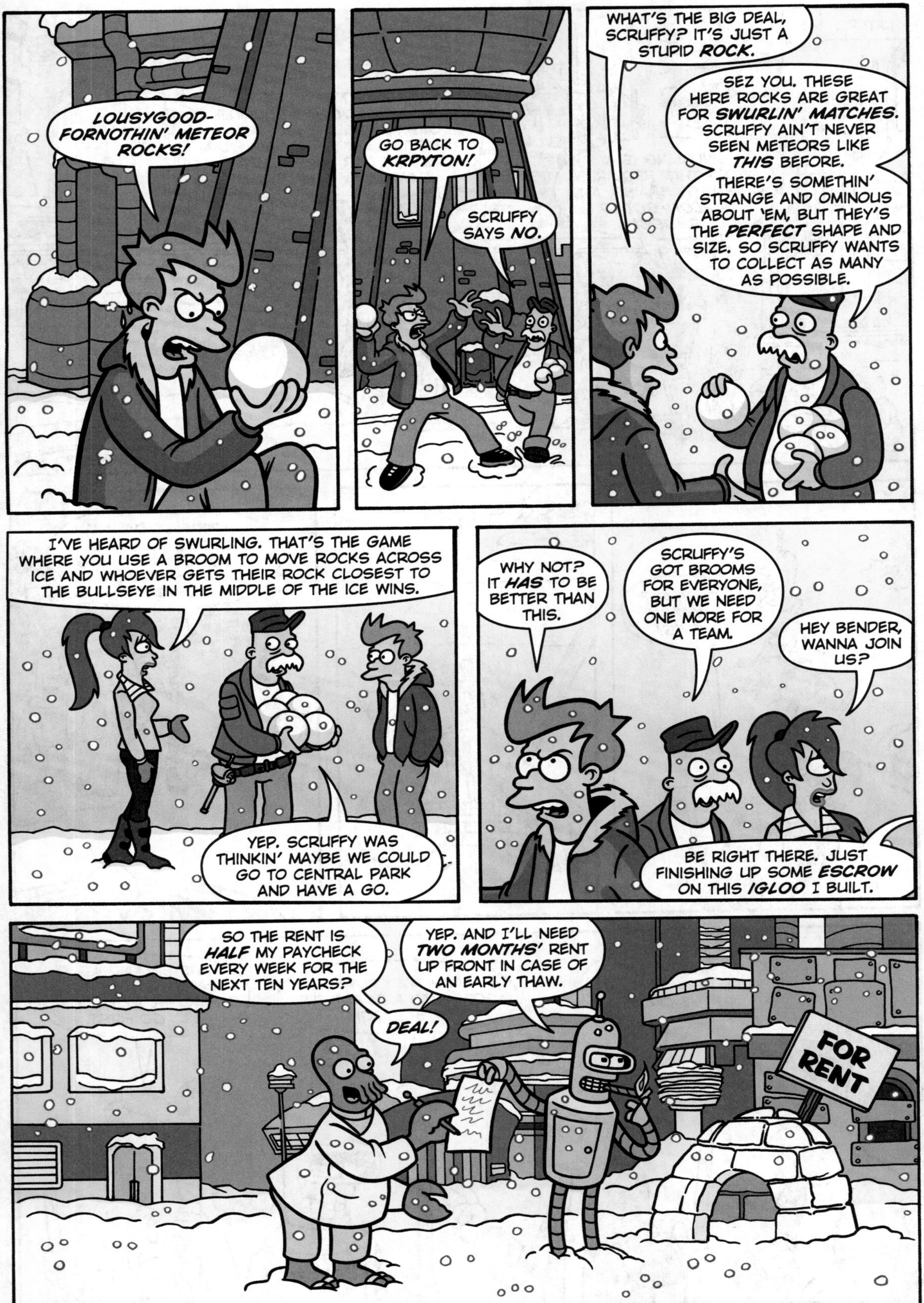
LOUSYGOOD-FORNOTHIN' METEOR ROCKS!
GO BACK TO KRPYTON!
SCRUFFY SAYS NO.
WHAT'S THE BIG DEAL, SCRUFFY? IT'S JUST A STUPID ROCK.
SEZ YOU. THESE HERE ROCKS ARE GREAT FOR SWURLIN' MATCHES. SCRUFFY AIN'T NEVER SEEN METEORS LIKE THIS BEFORE.
THERE'S SOMETHIN' STRANGE AND OMINOUS ABOUT 'EM, BUT THEY'S THE PERFECT SHAPE AND SIZE. SO SCRUFFY WANTS TO COLLECT AS MANY AS POSSIBLE.
I'VE HEARD OF SWURLING. THAT'S THE GAME WHERE YOU USE A BROOM TO MOVE ROCKS ACROSS ICE AND WHOEVER GETS THEIR ROCK CLOSEST TO THE BULLSEYE IN THE MIDDLE OF THE ICE WINS.
YEP. SCRUFFY WAS THINKIN' MAYBE WE COULD GO TO CENTRAL PARK AND HAVE A GO.
WHY NOT? IT HAS TO BE BETTER THAN THIS.
SCRUFFY'S GOT BROOMS FOR EVERYONE, BUT WE NEED ONE MORE FOR A TEAM.
HEY BENDER, WANNA JOIN US?
BE RIGHT THERE. JUST FINISHING UP SOME ESCROW ON THIS IGLOO I BUILT.
SO THE RENT IS HALF MY PAYCHECK EVERY WEEK FOR THE NEXT TEN YEARS?
YEP. AND I'LL NEED TWO MONTHS' RENT UP FRONT IN CASE OF AN EARLY THAW.
DEAL!
FOR RENT

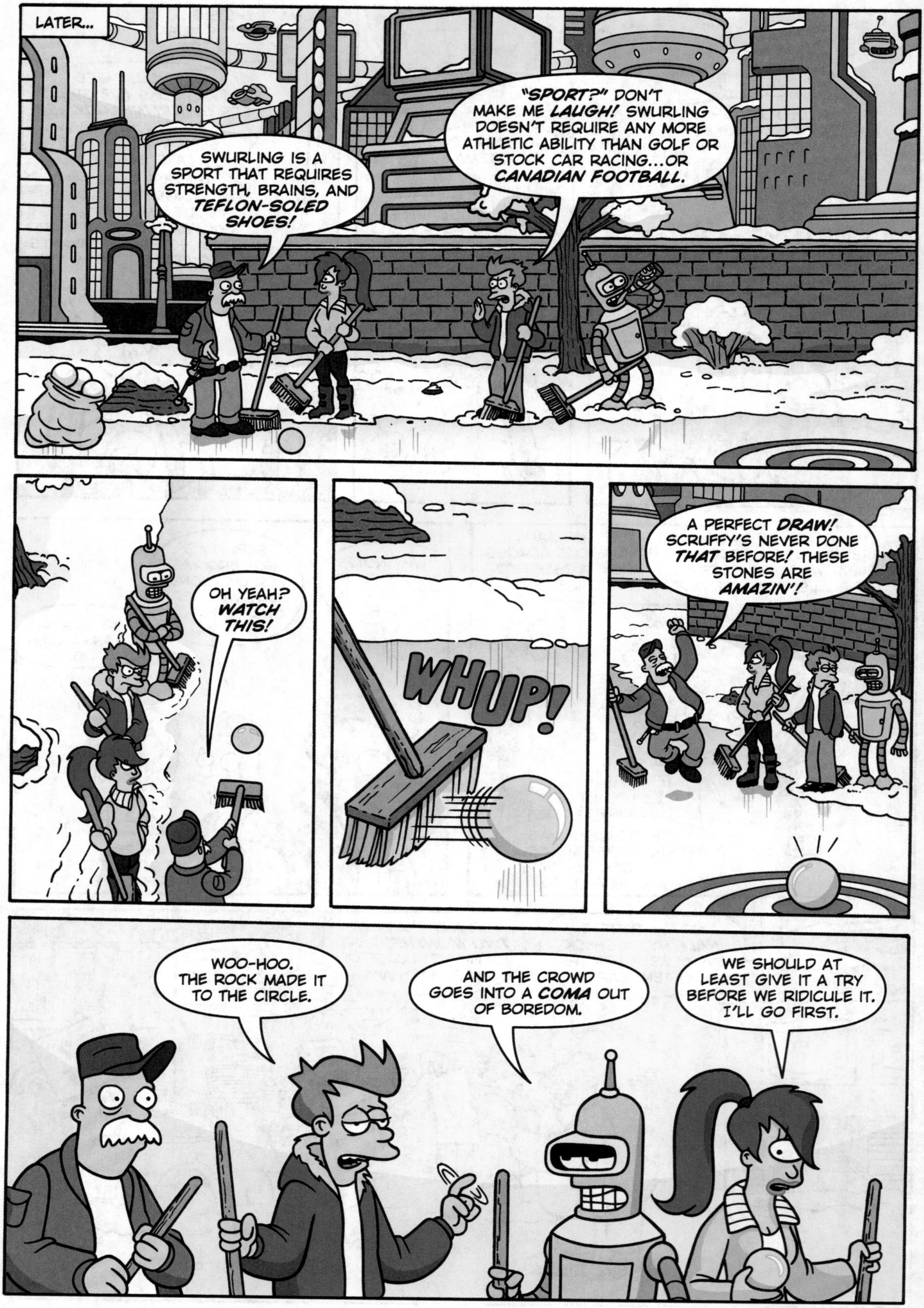
LATER...
SWURLING IS A SPORT THAT REQUIRES STRENGTH, BRAINS, AND TEFLON-SOLED SHOES!
"SPORT?" DON'T MAKE ME LAUGH! SWURLING DOESN'T REQUIRE ANY MORE ATHLETIC ABILITY THAN GOLF OR STOCK CAR RACING...OR CANADIAN FOOTBALL.
OH YEAH? WATCH THIS!
WHUP!
A PERFECT DRAW! SCRUFFY'S NEVER DONE THAT BEFORE! THESE STONES ARE AMAZIN'!
WOO-HOO. THE ROCK MADE IT TO THE CIRCLE.
AND THE CROWD GOES INTO A COMA OUT OF BOREDOM.
WE SHOULD AT LEAST GIVE IT A TRY BEFORE WE RIDICULE IT. I'LL GO FIRST.

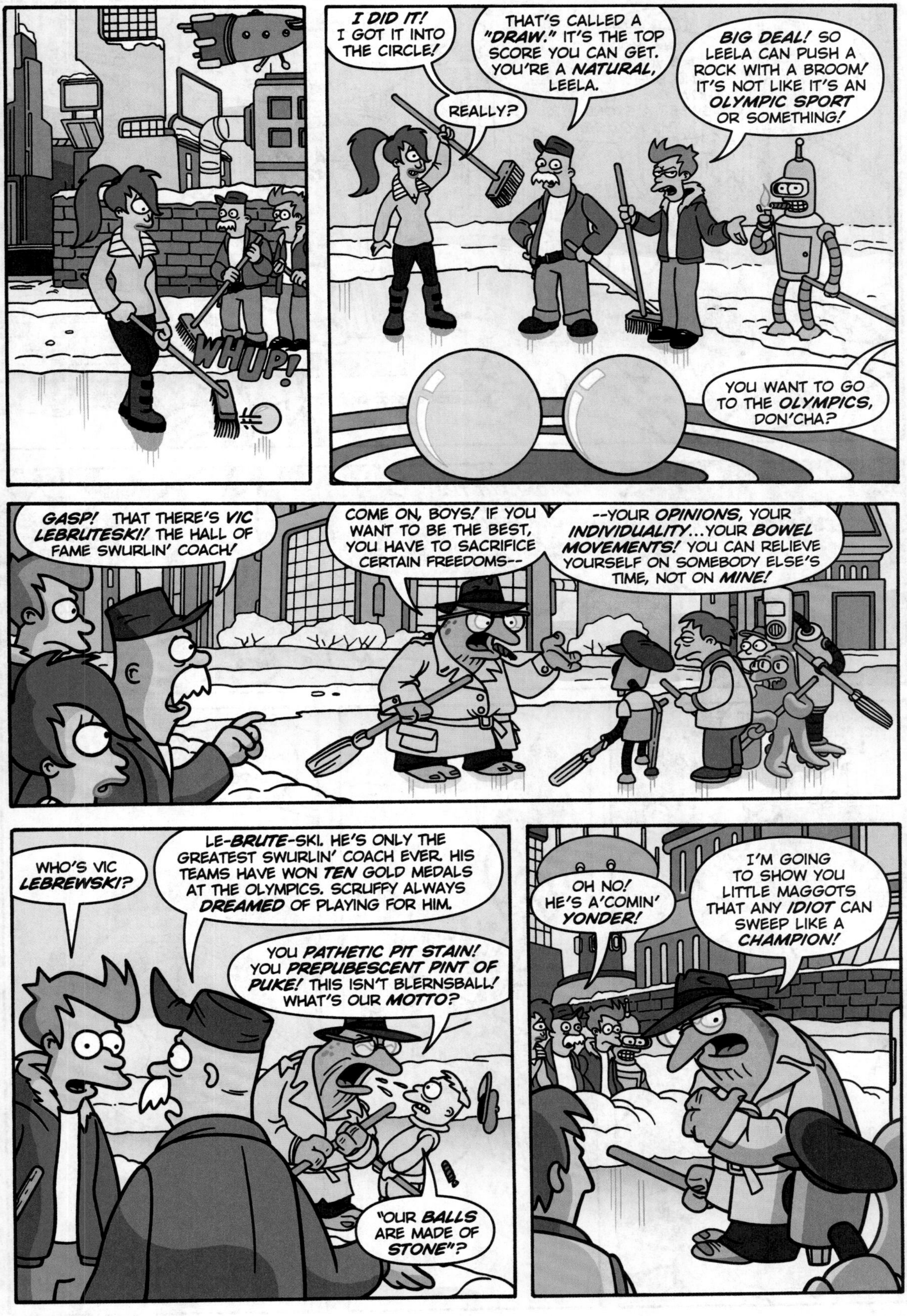
WHUP!
I DID IT! I GOT IT INTO THE CIRCLE!
THAT'S CALLED A "DRAW." IT'S THE TOP SCORE YOU CAN GET. YOU'RE A NATURAL, LEELA.
REALLY?
BIG DEAL! SO LEELA CAN PUSH A ROCK WITH A BROOM! IT'S NOT LIKE IT'S AN OLYMPIC SPORT OR SOMETHING!
YOU WANT TO GO TO THE OLYMPICS, DON'CHA?
GASP! THAT THERE'S VIC LEBRUTESKI! THE HALL OF FAME SWURLIN' COACH!
COME ON, BOYS! IF YOU WANT TO BE THE BEST, YOU HAVE TO SACRIFICE CERTAIN FREEDOMS--
--YOUR OPINIONS, YOUR INDIVIDUALITY...YOUR BOWEL MOVEMENTS! YOU CAN RELIEVE YOURSELF ON SOMEBODY ELSE'S TIME, NOT ON MINE!
WHO'S VIC LEBREWSKI?
LE-BRUTE-SKI. HE'S ONLY THE GREATEST SWURLIN' COACH EVER. HIS TEAMS HAVE WON TEN GOLD MEDALS AT THE OLYMPICS. SCRUFFY ALWAYS DREAMED OF PLAYING FOR HIM.
YOU PATHETIC PIT STAIN! YOU PREPUBESCENT PINT OF PUKE! THIS ISN'T BLERNSBALL! WHAT'S OUR MOTTO?
"OUR BALLS ARE MADE OF STONE"?
OH NO! HE'S A'COMIN' YONDER!
I'M GOING TO SHOW YOU LITTLE MAGGOTS THAT ANY IDIOT CAN SWEEP LIKE A CHAMPION!

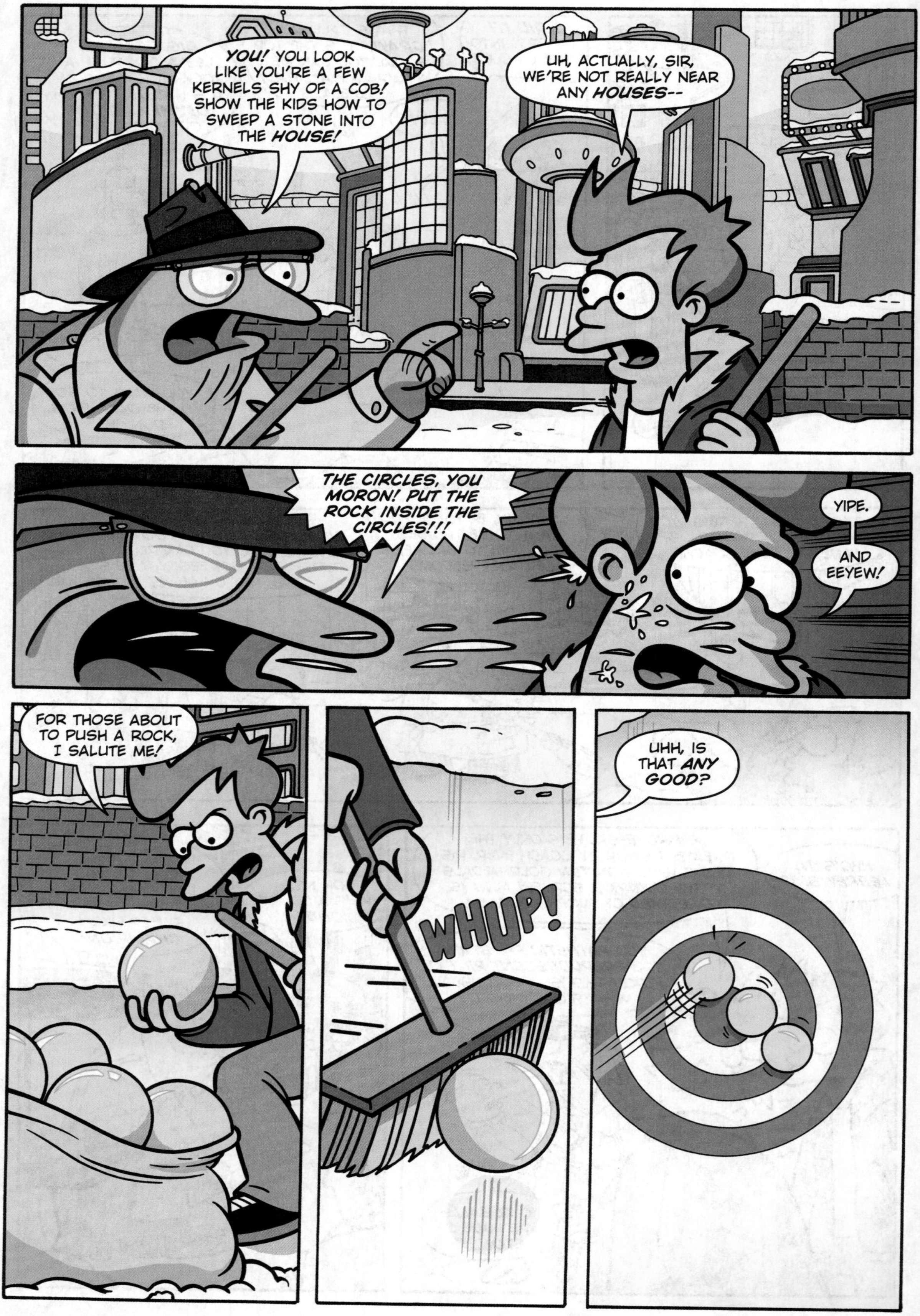
YOU! YOU LOOK LIKE YOU'RE A FEW KERNELS SHY OF A COB! SHOW THE KIDS HOW TO SWEEP A STONE INTO THE HOUSE!
UH, ACTUALLY, SIR, WE'RE NOT REALLY NEAR ANY HOUSES--
THE CIRCLES, YOU MORON! PUT THE ROCK INSIDE THE CIRCLES!!!
YIPE.
AND EEYEW!
FOR THOSE ABOUT TO PUSH A ROCK, I SALUTE ME!
WHUP!
UHH, IS THAT ANY GOOD?

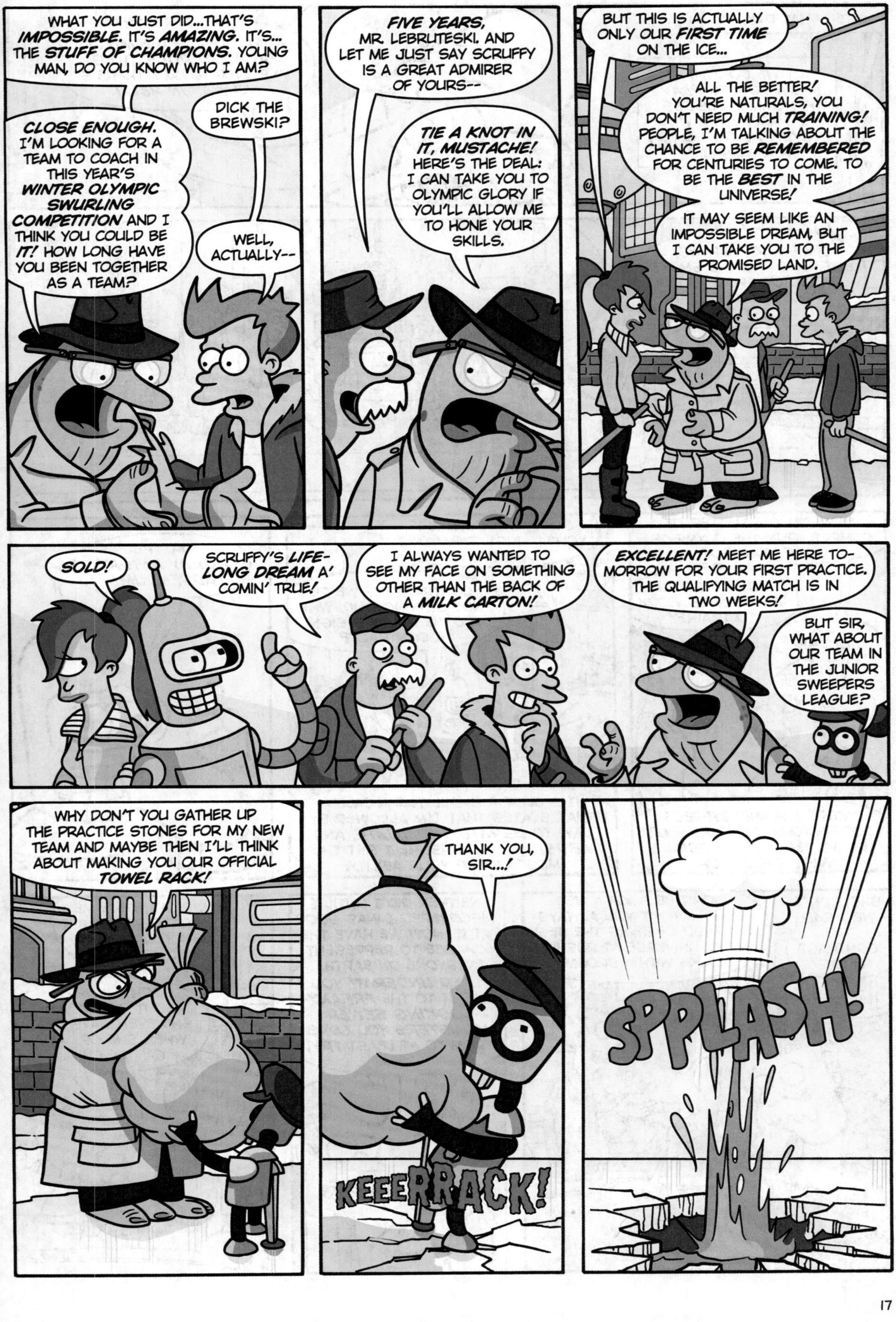
WHAT YOU JUST DID...THAT'S IMPOSSIBLE. IT'S AMAZING. IT'S... THE STUFF OF CHAMPIONS. YOUNG MAN, DO YOU KNOW WHO I AM?
DICK THE BREWSKI?
CLOSE ENOUGH. I'M LOOKING FOR A TEAM TO COACH IN THIS YEAR'S WINTER OLYMPIC SWURLING COMPETITION AND I THINK YOU COULD BE IT! HOW LONG HAVE YOU BEEN TOGETHER AS A TEAM?
WELL, ACTUALLY--
FIVE YEARS, MR. LEBRUTESKI. AND LET ME JUST SAY SCRUFFY IS A GREAT ADMIRER OF YOURS--
TIE A KNOT IN IT, MUSTACHE! HERE'S THE DEAL: I CAN TAKE YOU TO OLYMPIC GLORY IF YOU'LL ALLOW ME TO HONE YOUR SKILLS.
BUT THIS IS ACTUALLY ONLY OUR FIRST TIME ON THE ICE...
ALL THE BETTER! YOU'RE NATURALS, YOU DON'T NEED MUCH TRAINING! PEOPLE, I'M TALKING ABOUT THE CHANCE TO BE REMEMBERED FOR CENTURIES TO COME. TO BE THE BEST IN THE UNIVERSE!
IT MAY SEEM LIKE AN IMPOSSIBLE DREAM, BUT I CAN TAKE YOU TO THE PROMISED LAND.
SOLD!
SCRUFFY'S LIFE-LONG DREAM A' COMIN' TRUE!
I ALWAYS WANTED TO SEE MY FACE ON SOMETHING OTHER THAN THE BACK OF A MILK CARTON!
EXCELLENT! MEET ME HERE TO-MORROW FOR YOUR FIRST PRACTICE. THE QUALIFYING MATCH IS IN TWO WEEKS!
BUT SIR, WHAT ABOUT OUR TEAM IN THE JUNIOR SWEEPERS LEAGUE?
WHY DON'T YOU GATHER UP THE PRACTICE STONES FOR MY NEW TEAM AND MAYBE THEN I'LL THINK ABOUT MAKING YOU OUR OFFICIAL TOWEL RACK!
THANK YOU, SIR...!
KEEERRACK!
SPPLASH!

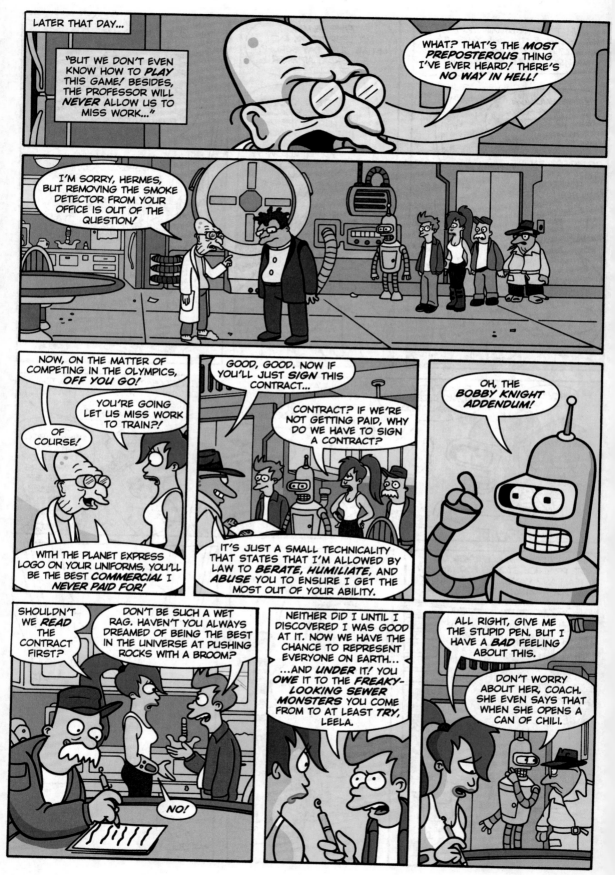

LATER THAT DAY...

"BUT WE DON'T EVEN KNOW HOW TO *PLAY* THIS GAME! BESIDES, THE PROFESSOR WILL *NEVER* ALLOW US TO MISS WORK..."

WHAT? THAT'S THE *MOST PREPOSTEROUS* THING I'VE EVER HEARD! THERE'S *NO WAY IN HELL!*

I'M SORRY, HERMES, BUT REMOVING THE SMOKE DETECTOR FROM YOUR OFFICE IS OUT OF THE QUESTION!

NOW, ON THE MATTER OF COMPETING IN THE OLYMPICS, *OFF YOU GO!*

YOU'RE GOING LET US MISS WORK TO TRAIN?!

OF COURSE!

WITH THE PLANET EXPRESS LOGO ON YOUR UNIFORMS, YOU'LL BE THE BEST *COMMERCIAL* I *NEVER PAID FOR!*

GOOD, GOOD. NOW IF YOU'LL JUST *SIGN* THIS CONTRACT...

CONTRACT? IF WE'RE NOT GETTING PAID, WHY DO WE HAVE TO SIGN A CONTRACT?

IT'S JUST A SMALL TECHNICALITY THAT STATES THAT I'M ALLOWED BY LAW TO *BERATE, HUMILIATE,* AND *ABUSE* YOU TO ENSURE I GET THE MOST OUT OF YOUR ABILITY.

OH, THE *BOBBY KNIGHT ADDENDUM!*

SHOULDN'T WE *READ* THE CONTRACT FIRST?

DON'T BE SUCH A WET RAG. HAVEN'T YOU ALWAYS DREAMED OF BEING THE BEST IN THE UNIVERSE AT PUSHING ROCKS WITH A BROOM?

NO!

NEITHER DID I UNTIL I DISCOVERED I WAS GOOD AT IT. NOW WE HAVE THE CHANCE TO REPRESENT EVERYONE ON EARTH...
...AND *UNDER* IT! YOU *OWE* IT TO THE *FREAKY-LOOKING SEWER MONSTERS* YOU COME FROM TO AT LEAST *TRY,* LEELA.

ALL RIGHT, GIVE ME THE STUPID PEN. BUT I HAVE A *BAD* FEELING ABOUT THIS.

DON'T WORRY ABOUT HER, COACH. SHE EVEN SAYS THAT WHEN SHE OPENS A CAN OF CHILI.

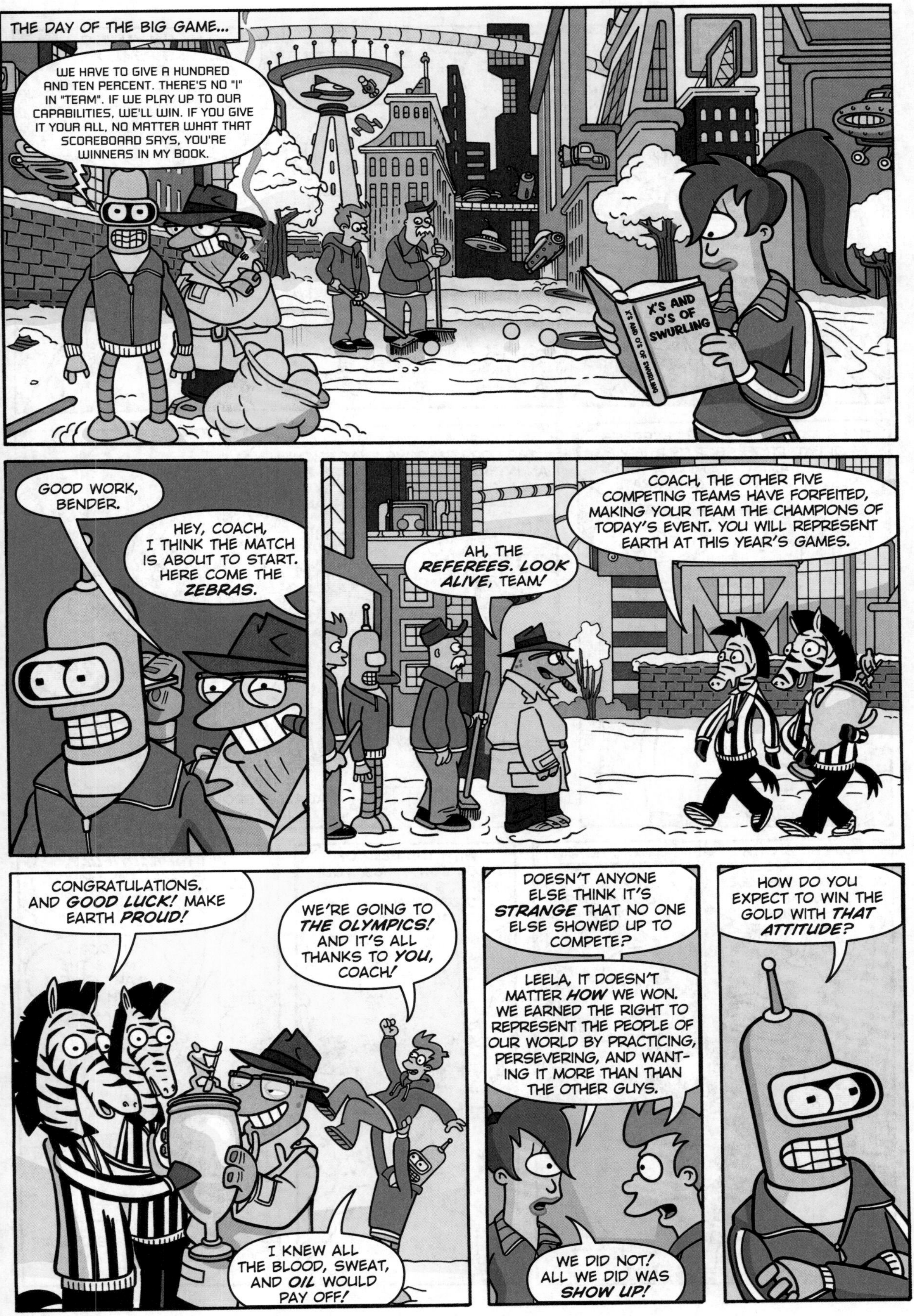
THE DAY OF THE BIG GAME...
WE HAVE TO GIVE A HUNDRED AND TEN PERCENT. THERE'S NO "I" IN "TEAM". IF WE PLAY UP TO OUR CAPABILITIES, WE'LL WIN. IF YOU GIVE IT YOUR ALL, NO MATTER WHAT THAT SCOREBOARD SAYS, YOU'RE WINNERS IN MY BOOK.
X'S AND O'S OF SWURLING
X'S AND O'S OF SWURLING
GOOD WORK, BENDER.
HEY, COACH, I THINK THE MATCH IS ABOUT TO START. HERE COME THE ZEBRAS.
AH, THE REFEREES. LOOK ALIVE, TEAM!
COACH, THE OTHER FIVE COMPETING TEAMS HAVE FORFEITED, MAKING YOUR TEAM THE CHAMPIONS OF TODAY'S EVENT. YOU WILL REPRESENT EARTH AT THIS YEAR'S GAMES.
CONGRATULATIONS. AND GOOD LUCK! MAKE EARTH PROUD!
WE'RE GOING TO THE OLYMPICS! AND IT'S ALL THANKS TO YOU, COACH!
I KNEW ALL THE BLOOD, SWEAT, AND OIL WOULD PAY OFF!
DOESN'T ANYONE ELSE THINK IT'S STRANGE THAT NO ONE ELSE SHOWED UP TO COMPETE?
LEELA, IT DOESN'T MATTER HOW WE WON. WE EARNED THE RIGHT TO REPRESENT THE PEOPLE OF OUR WORLD BY PRACTICING, PERSEVERING, AND WANTING IT MORE THAN THAN THE OTHER GUYS.
WE DID NOT! ALL WE DID WAS SHOW UP!
HOW DO YOU EXPECT TO WIN THE GOLD WITH THAT ATTITUDE?

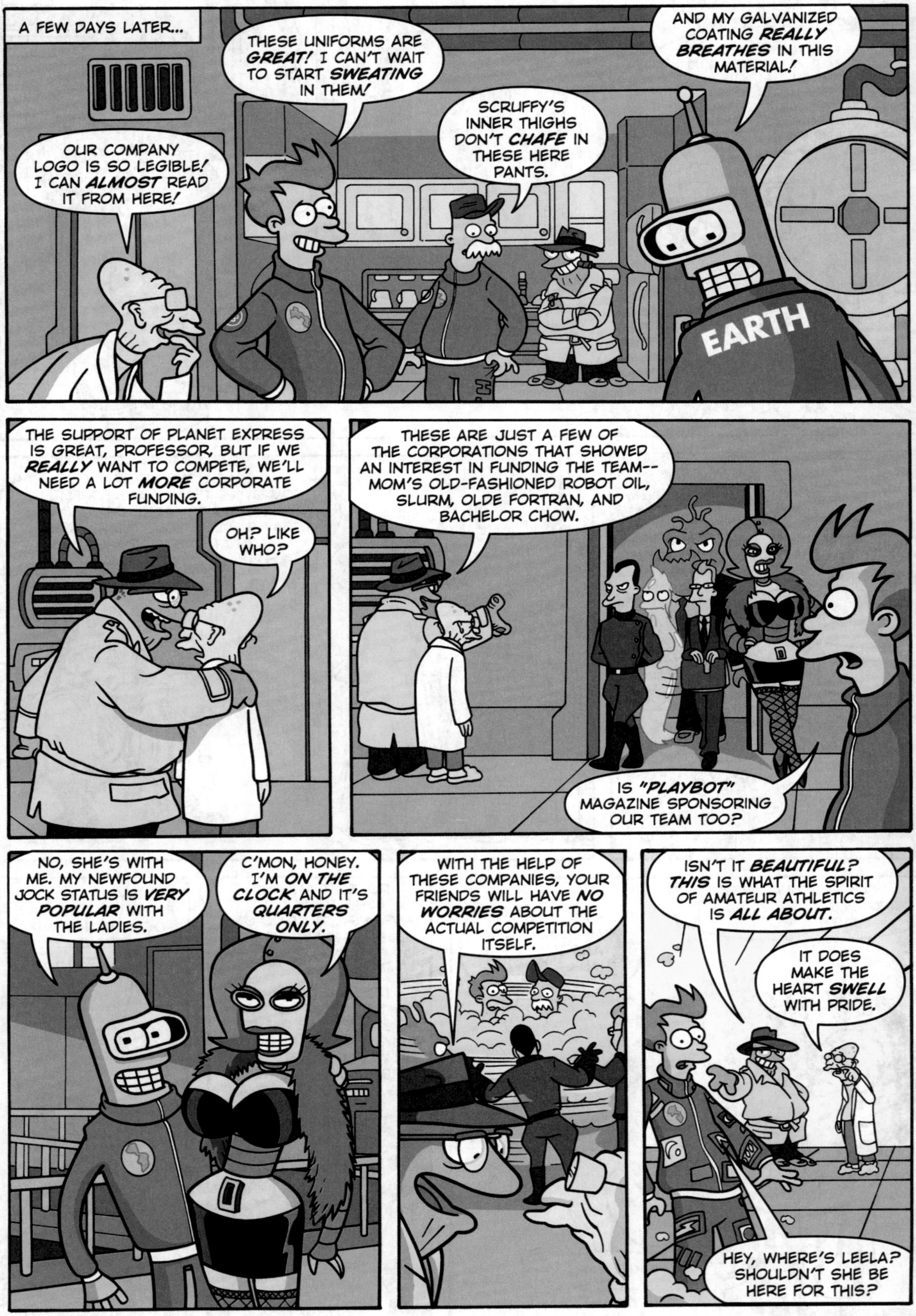
A FEW DAYS LATER...
THESE UNIFORMS ARE GREAT! I CAN'T WAIT TO START SWEATING IN THEM!
AND MY GALVANIZED COATING REALLY BREATHES IN THIS MATERIAL!
SCRUFFY'S INNER THIGHS DON'T CHAFE IN THESE HERE PANTS.
OUR COMPANY LOGO IS SO LEGIBLE! I CAN ALMOST READ IT FROM HERE!
EARTH
THE SUPPORT OF PLANET EXPRESS IS GREAT, PROFESSOR, BUT IF WE REALLY WANT TO COMPETE, WE'LL NEED A LOT MORE CORPORATE FUNDING.
OH? LIKE WHO?
THESE ARE JUST A FEW OF THE CORPORATIONS THAT SHOWED AN INTEREST IN FUNDING THE TEAM-- MOM'S OLD-FASHIONED ROBOT OIL, SLURM, OLDE FORTRAN, AND BACHELOR CHOW.
IS "PLAYBOT" MAGAZINE SPONSORING OUR TEAM TOO?
NO, SHE'S WITH ME. MY NEWFOUND JOCK STATUS IS VERY POPULAR WITH THE LADIES.
C'MON, HONEY. I'M ON THE CLOCK AND IT'S QUARTERS ONLY.
WITH THE HELP OF THESE COMPANIES, YOUR FRIENDS WILL HAVE NO WORRIES ABOUT THE ACTUAL COMPETITION ITSELF.
ISN'T IT BEAUTIFUL? THIS IS WHAT THE SPIRIT OF AMATEUR ATHLETICS IS ALL ABOUT.
IT DOES MAKE THE HEART SWELL WITH PRIDE.
HEY, WHERE'S LEELA? SHOULDN'T SHE BE HERE FOR THIS?

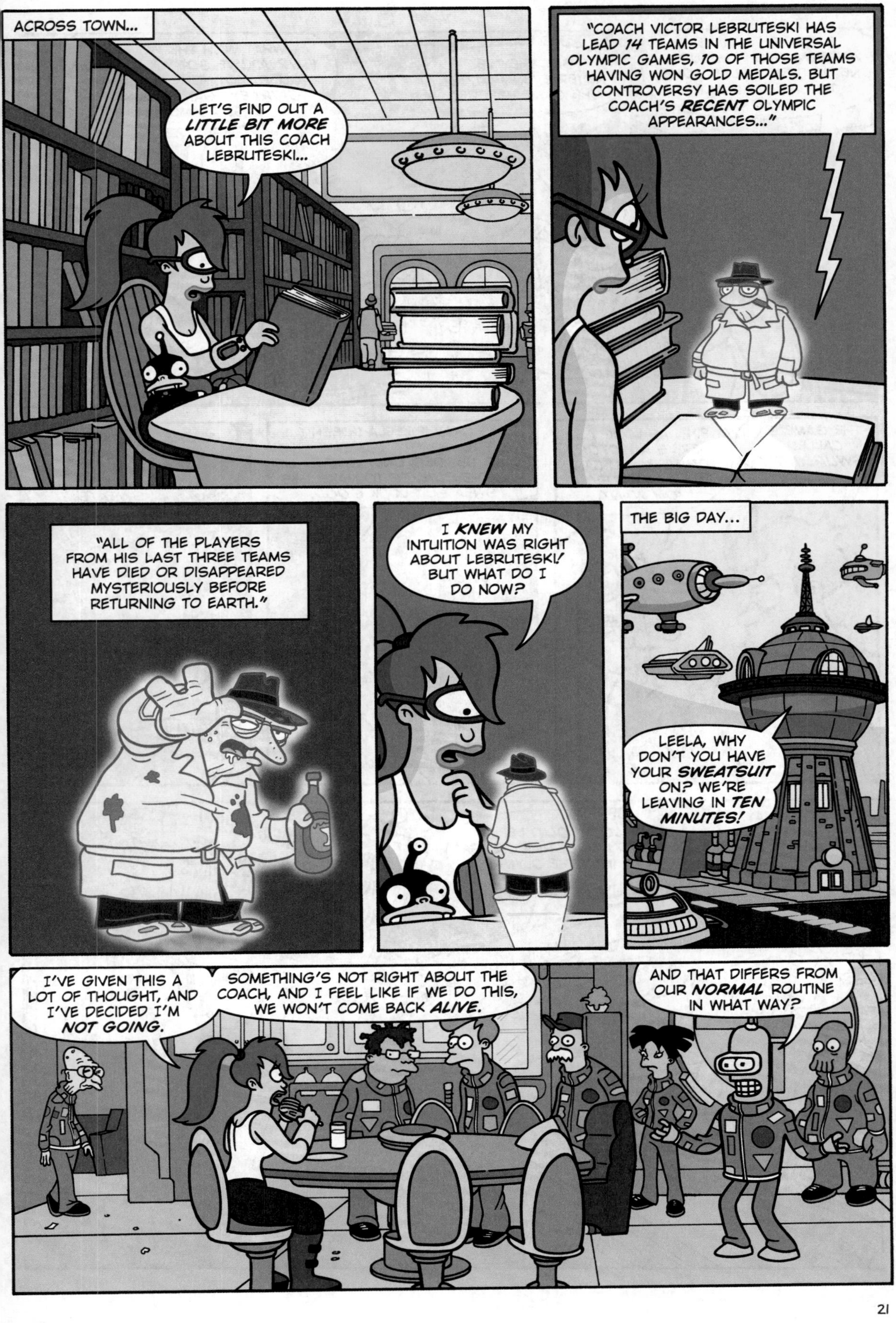
ACROSS TOWN...
LET'S FIND OUT A LITTLE BIT MORE ABOUT THIS COACH LEBRUTESKI...
"COACH VICTOR LEBRUTESKI HAS LEAD 14 TEAMS IN THE UNIVERSAL OLYMPIC GAMES, 10 OF THOSE TEAMS HAVING WON GOLD MEDALS. BUT CONTROVERSY HAS SOILED THE COACH'S RECENT OLYMPIC APPEARANCES..."
"ALL OF THE PLAYERS FROM HIS LAST THREE TEAMS HAVE DIED OR DISAPPEARED MYSTERIOUSLY BEFORE RETURNING TO EARTH."
I KNEW MY INTUITION WAS RIGHT ABOUT LEBRUTESKI! BUT WHAT DO I DO NOW?
THE BIG DAY...
LEELA, WHY DON'T YOU HAVE YOUR SWEATSUIT ON? WE'RE LEAVING IN TEN MINUTES!
I'VE GIVEN THIS A LOT OF THOUGHT, AND I'VE DECIDED I'M NOT GOING.
SOMETHING'S NOT RIGHT ABOUT THE COACH, AND I FEEL LIKE IF WE DO THIS, WE WON'T COME BACK ALIVE.
AND THAT DIFFERS FROM OUR NORMAL ROUTINE IN WHAT WAY?

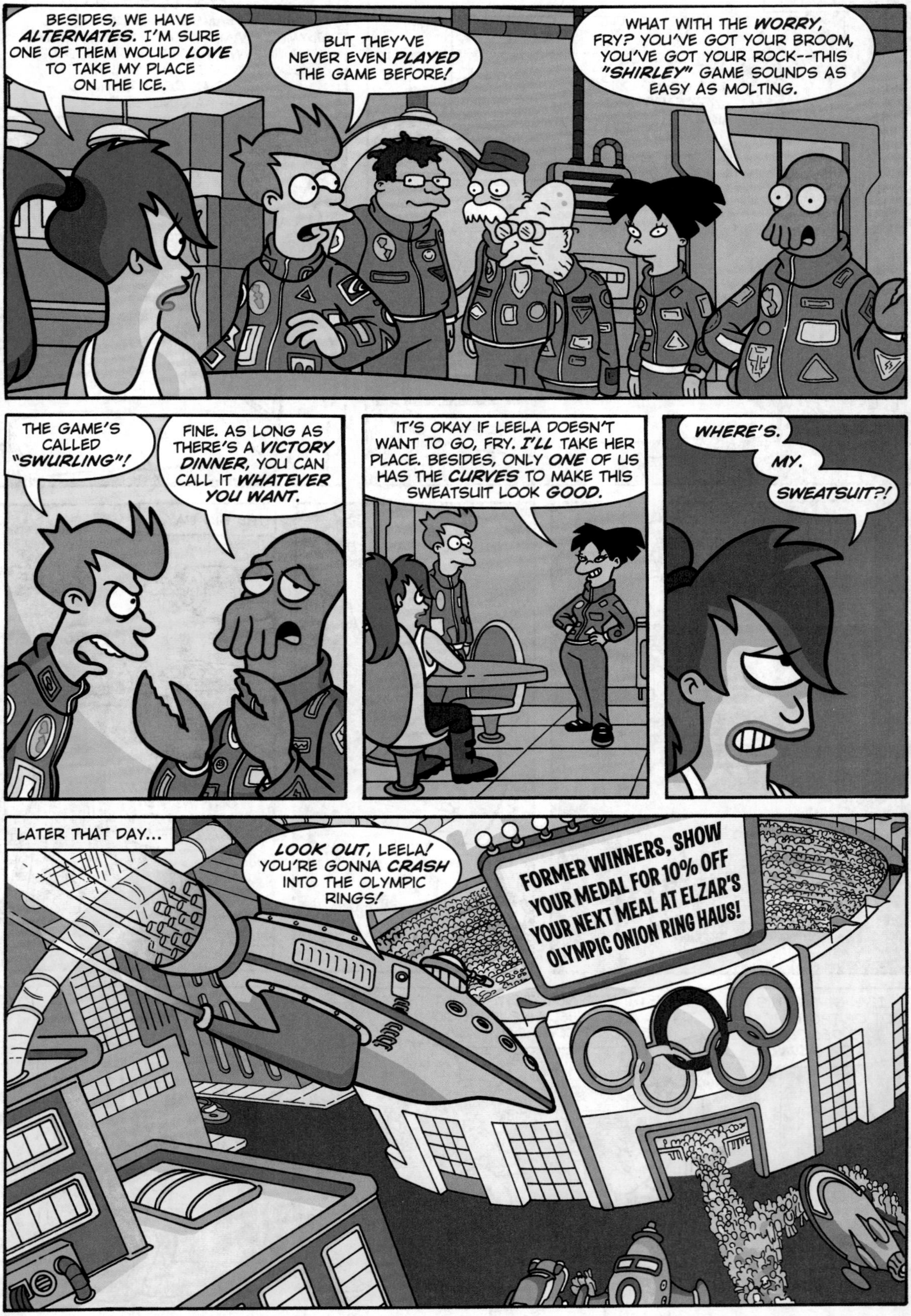
BESIDES, WE HAVE ALTERNATES. I'M SURE ONE OF THEM WOULD LOVE TO TAKE MY PLACE ON THE ICE.
BUT THEY'VE NEVER EVEN PLAYED THE GAME BEFORE!
WHAT WITH THE WORRY, FRY? YOU'VE GOT YOUR BROOM, YOU'VE GOT YOUR ROCK--THIS "SHIRLEY" GAME SOUNDS AS EASY AS MOLTING.
THE GAME'S CALLED "SWURLING"!
FINE. AS LONG AS THERE'S A VICTORY DINNER, YOU CAN CALL IT WHATEVER YOU WANT.
IT'S OKAY IF LEELA DOESN'T WANT TO GO, FRY. I'LL TAKE HER PLACE. BESIDES, ONLY ONE OF US HAS THE CURVES TO MAKE THIS SWEATSUIT LOOK GOOD.
WHERE'S.
MY.
SWEATSUIT?!
LATER THAT DAY...
LOOK OUT, LEELA! YOU'RE GONNA CRASH INTO THE OLYMPIC RINGS!
FORMER WINNERS, SHOW YOUR MEDAL FOR 10% OFF YOUR NEXT MEAL AT ELZAR'S OLYMPIC ONION RING HAUS!

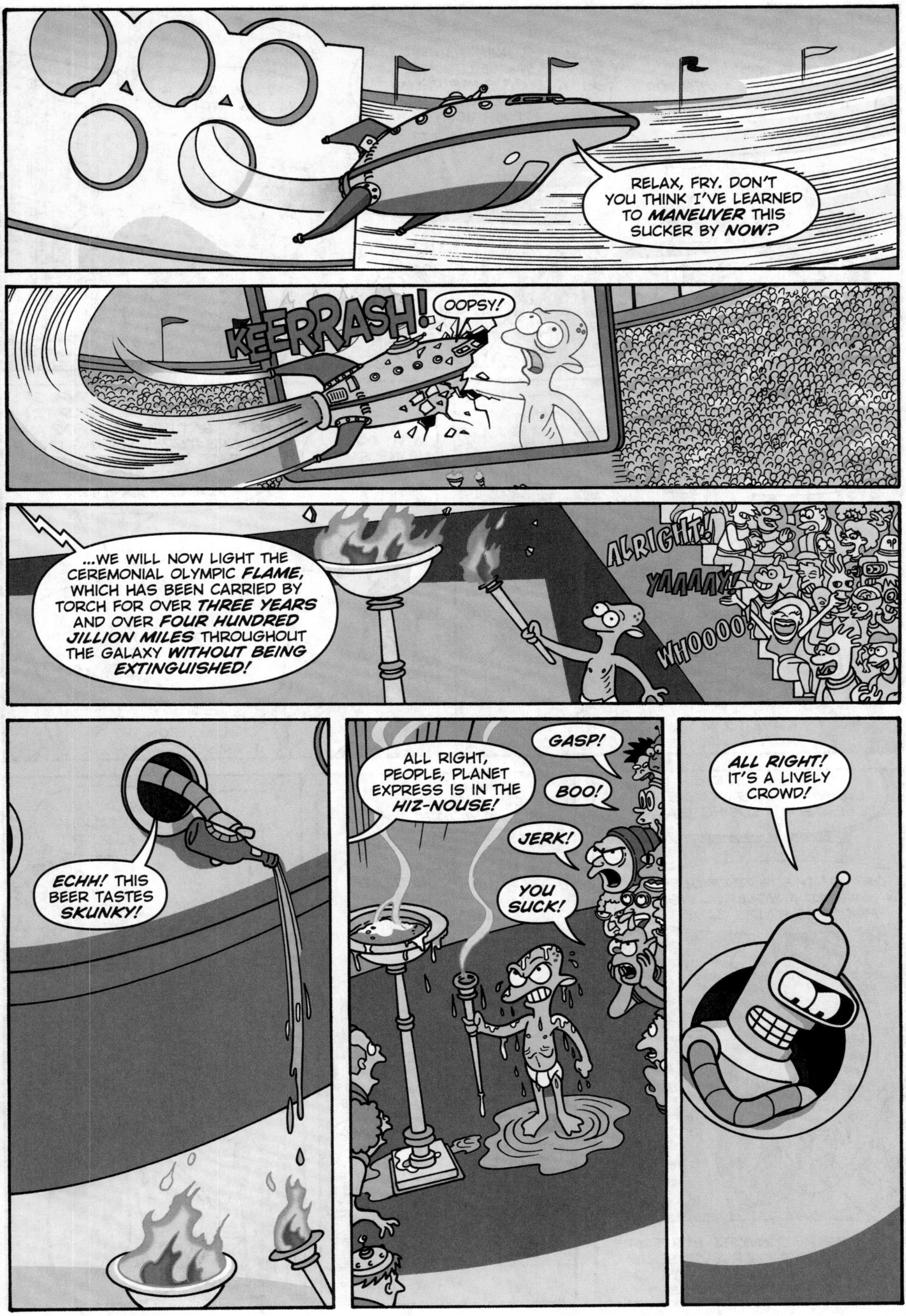
RELAX, FRY. DON'T YOU THINK I'VE LEARNED TO MANEUVER THIS SUCKER BY NOW?
KEERRASH!
OOPSY!
...WE WILL NOW LIGHT THE CEREMONIAL OLYMPIC FLAME, WHICH HAS BEEN CARRIED BY TORCH FOR OVER THREE YEARS AND OVER FOUR HUNDRED JILLION MILES THROUGHOUT THE GALAXY WITHOUT BEING EXTINGUISHED!
ALRIGHT!
YAAAAY!
WHOOOO!
ECHH! THIS BEER TASTES SKUNKY!
ALL RIGHT, PEOPLE, PLANET EXPRESS IS IN THE HIZ-NOUSE!
GASP!
BOO!
JERK!
YOU SUCK!
ALL RIGHT! IT'S A LIVELY CROWD!

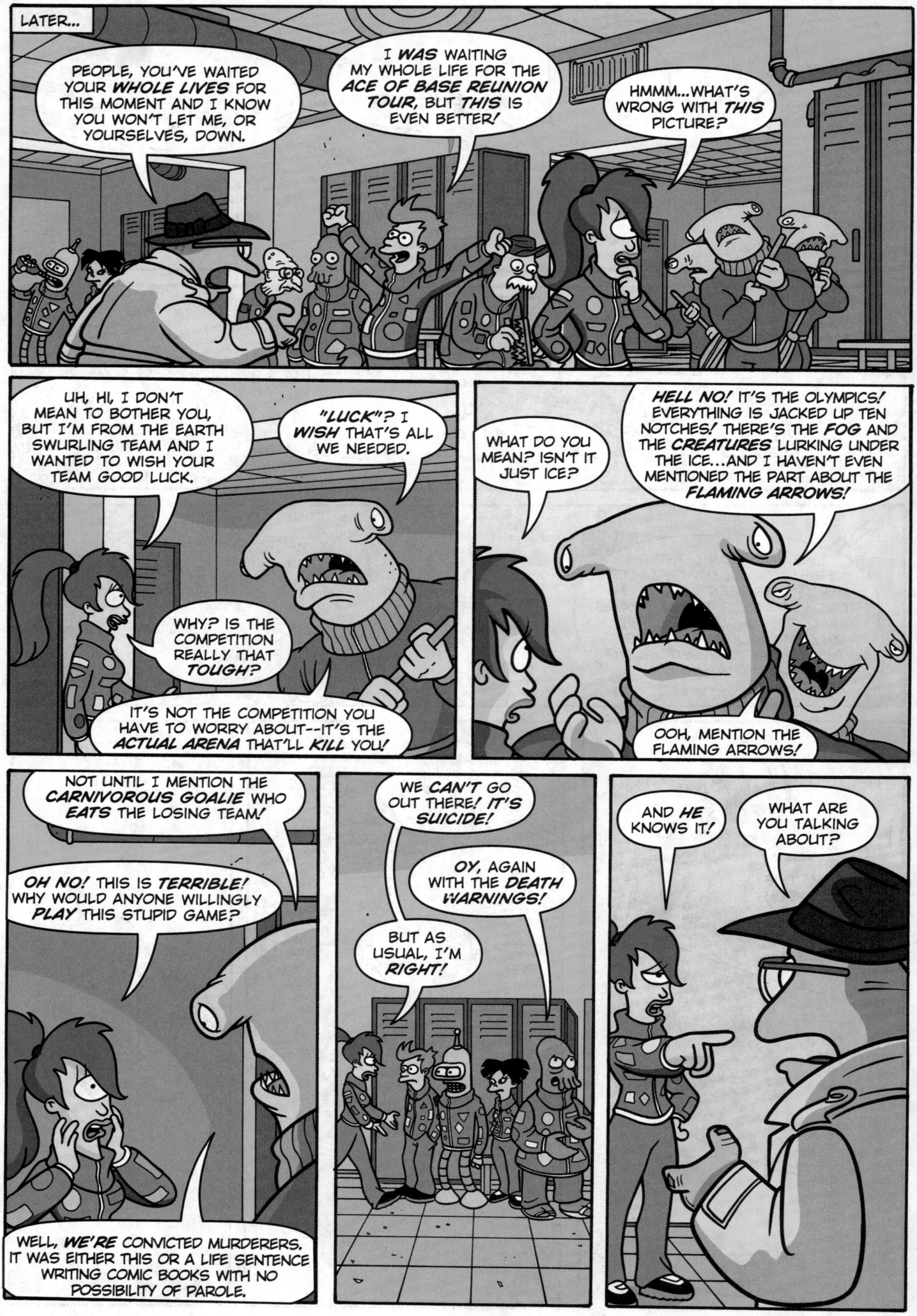
LATER...
PEOPLE, YOU'VE WAITED YOUR WHOLE LIVES FOR THIS MOMENT AND I KNOW YOU WON'T LET ME, OR YOURSELVES, DOWN.
I WAS WAITING MY WHOLE LIFE FOR THE ACE OF BASE REUNION TOUR, BUT THIS IS EVEN BETTER!
HMMM...WHAT'S WRONG WITH THIS PICTURE?
UH, HI, I DON'T MEAN TO BOTHER YOU, BUT I'M FROM THE EARTH SWURLING TEAM AND I WANTED TO WISH YOUR TEAM GOOD LUCK.
"LUCK"? I WISH THAT'S ALL WE NEEDED.
WHY? IS THE COMPETITION REALLY THAT TOUGH?
IT'S NOT THE COMPETITION YOU HAVE TO WORRY ABOUT--IT'S THE ACTUAL ARENA THAT'LL KILL YOU!
WHAT DO YOU MEAN? ISN'T IT JUST ICE?
HELL NO! IT'S THE OLYMPICS! EVERYTHING IS JACKED UP TEN NOTCHES! THERE'S THE FOG AND THE CREATURES LURKING UNDER THE ICE...AND I HAVEN'T EVEN MENTIONED THE PART ABOUT THE FLAMING ARROWS!
OOH, MENTION THE FLAMING ARROWS!
NOT UNTIL I MENTION THE CARNIVOROUS GOALIE WHO EATS THE LOSING TEAM!
OH NO! THIS IS TERRIBLE! WHY WOULD ANYONE WILLINGLY PLAY THIS STUPID GAME?
WELL, WE'RE CONVICTED MURDERERS. IT WAS EITHER THIS OR A LIFE SENTENCE WRITING COMIC BOOKS WITH NO POSSIBILITY OF PAROLE.
WE CAN'T GO OUT THERE! IT'S SUICIDE!
OY, AGAIN WITH THE DEATH WARNINGS!
BUT AS USUAL, I'M RIGHT!
AND HE KNOWS IT!
WHAT ARE YOU TALKING ABOUT?

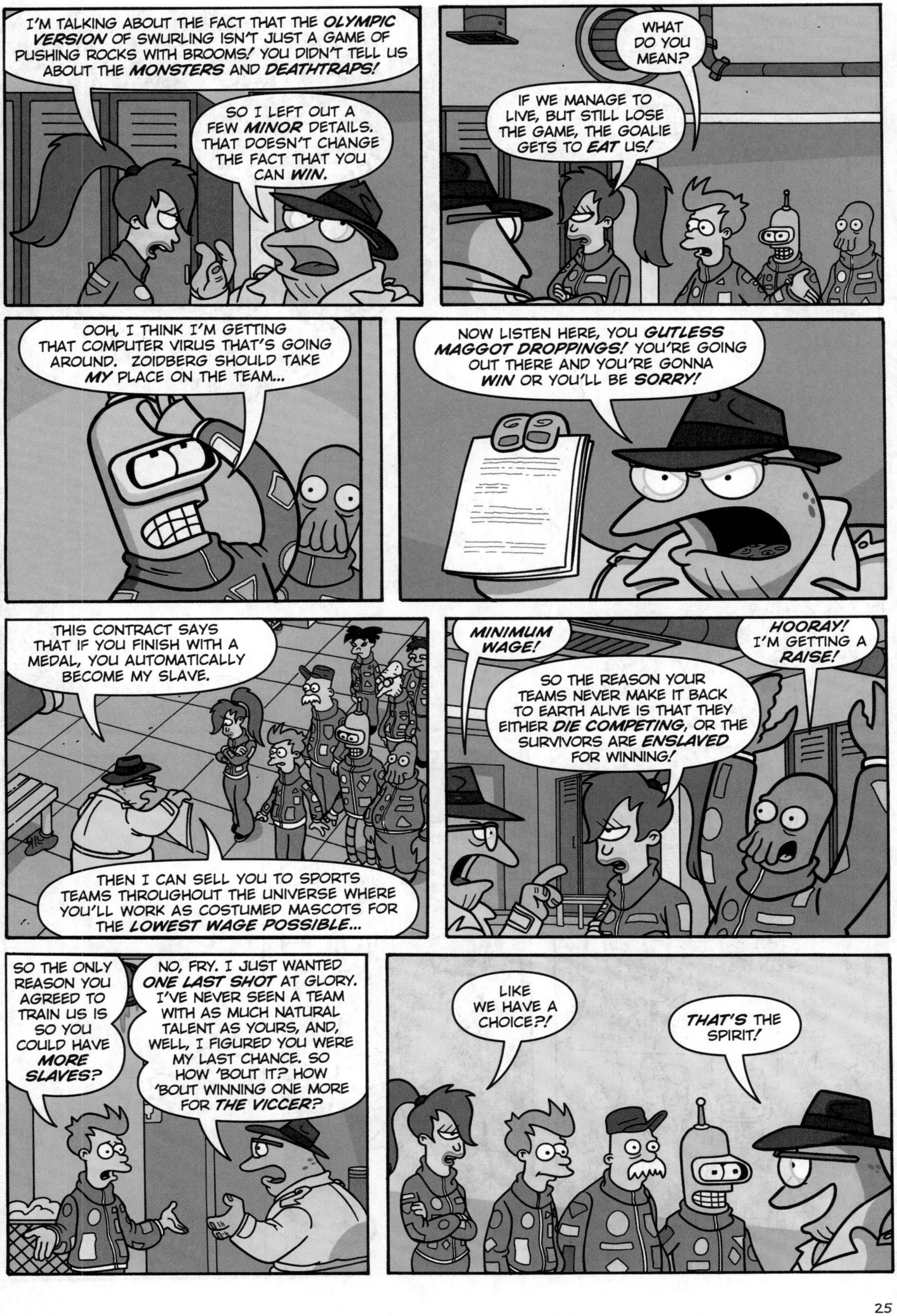
I'M TALKING ABOUT THE FACT THAT THE OLYMPIC VERSION OF SWURLING ISN'T JUST A GAME OF PUSHING ROCKS WITH BROOMS! YOU DIDN'T TELL US ABOUT THE MONSTERS AND DEATHTRAPS!
SO I LEFT OUT A FEW MINOR DETAILS. THAT DOESN'T CHANGE THE FACT THAT YOU CAN WIN.
WHAT DO YOU MEAN?
IF WE MANAGE TO LIVE, BUT STILL LOSE THE GAME, THE GOALIE GETS TO EAT US!
OOH, I THINK I'M GETTING THAT COMPUTER VIRUS THAT'S GOING AROUND. ZOIDBERG SHOULD TAKE MY PLACE ON THE TEAM...
NOW LISTEN HERE, YOU GUTLESS MAGGOT DROPPINGS! YOU'RE GOING OUT THERE AND YOU'RE GONNA WIN OR YOU'LL BE SORRY!
THIS CONTRACT SAYS THAT IF YOU FINISH WITH A MEDAL, YOU AUTOMATICALLY BECOME MY SLAVE.
THEN I CAN SELL YOU TO SPORTS TEAMS THROUGHOUT THE UNIVERSE WHERE YOU'LL WORK AS COSTUMED MASCOTS FOR THE LOWEST WAGE POSSIBLE...
MINIMUM WAGE!
HOORAY! I'M GETTING A RAISE!
SO THE REASON YOUR TEAMS NEVER MAKE IT BACK TO EARTH ALIVE IS THAT THEY EITHER DIE COMPETING, OR THE SURVIVORS ARE ENSLAVED FOR WINNING!
SO THE ONLY REASON YOU AGREED TO TRAIN US IS SO YOU COULD HAVE MORE SLAVES?
NO, FRY. I JUST WANTED ONE LAST SHOT AT GLORY. I'VE NEVER SEEN A TEAM WITH AS MUCH NATURAL TALENT AS YOURS, AND, WELL, I FIGURED YOU WERE MY LAST CHANCE. SO HOW 'BOUT IT? HOW 'BOUT WINNING ONE MORE FOR THE VICCER?
LIKE WE HAVE A CHOICE?!
THAT'S THE SPIRIT!

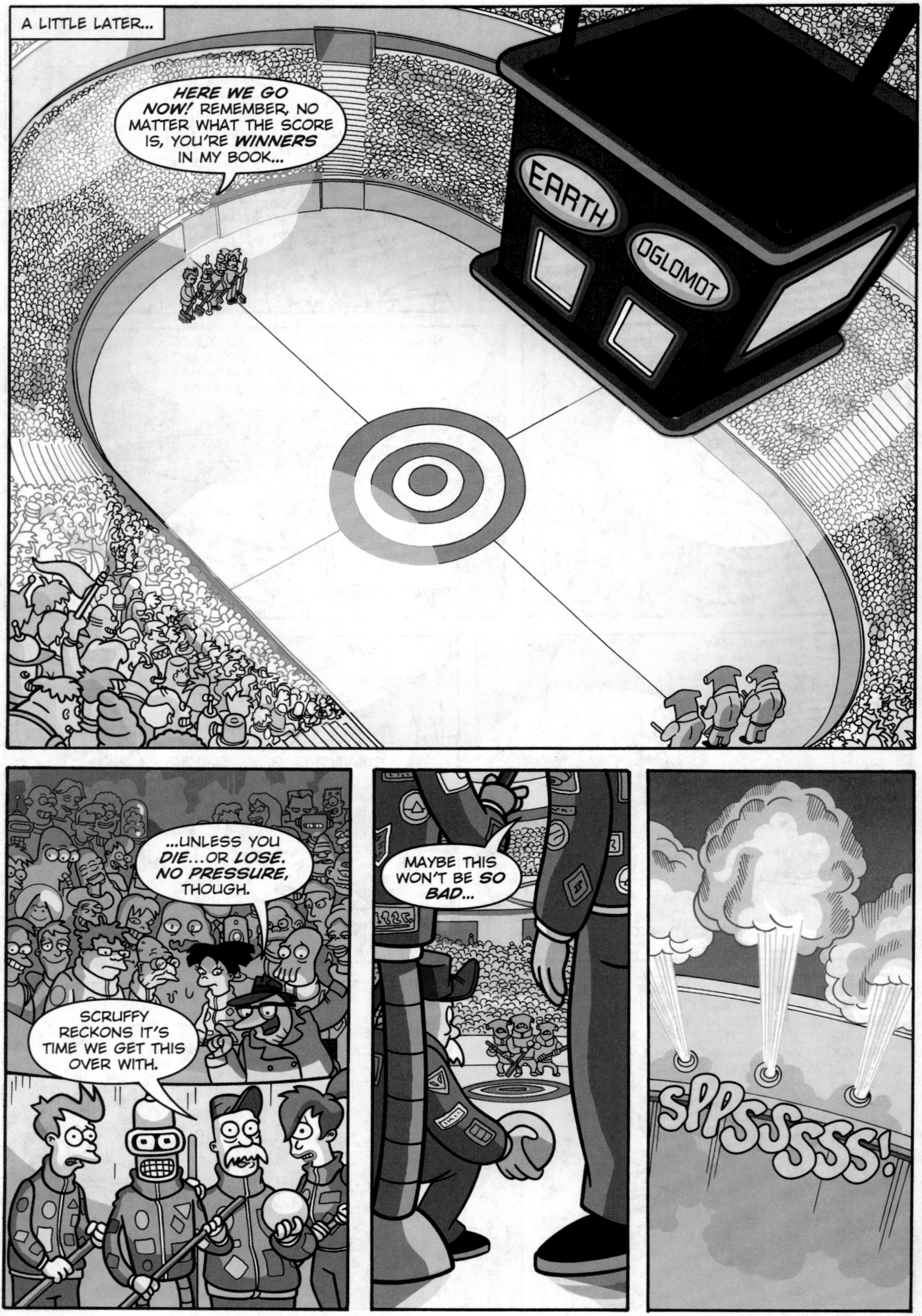

A LITTLE LATER...
HERE WE GO NOW! REMEMBER, NO MATTER WHAT THE SCORE IS, YOU'RE WINNERS IN MY BOOK...
EARTH
OGLOMOT
...UNLESS YOU DIE...OR LOSE. NO PRESSURE, THOUGH.
SCRUFFY RECKONS IT'S TIME WE GET THIS OVER WITH.
MAYBE THIS WON'T BE SO BAD...
SPPSSSSSS!

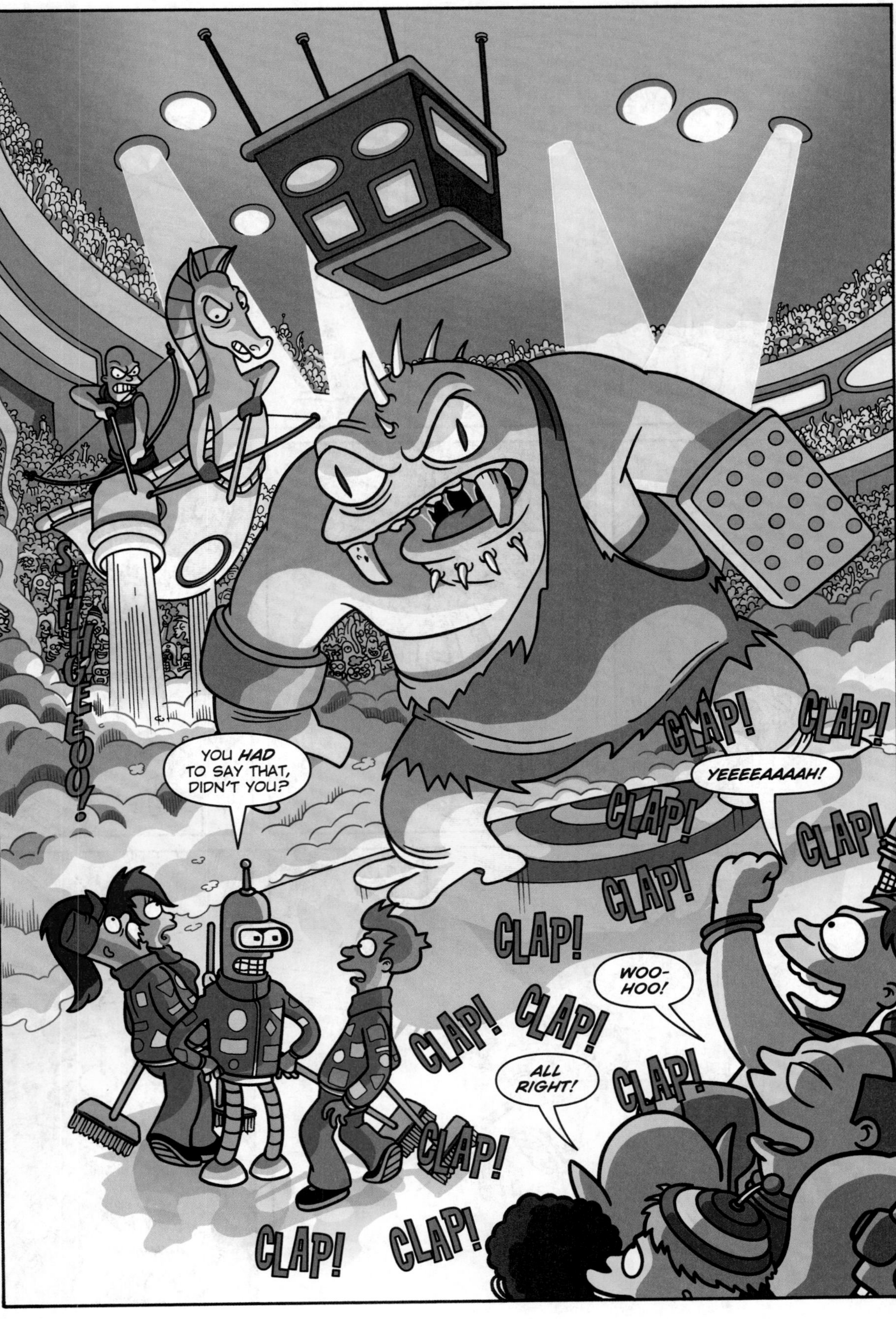
SHHHGEEOOO!
YOU *HAD* TO SAY THAT, DIDN'T YOU?
CLAP! CLAP!
YEEEEAAAAH!
CLAP!
CLAP!
CLAP!
CLAP!
WOO-HOO!
CLAP! CLAP!
ALL RIGHT!
CLAP!
CLAP!
CLAP! CLAP!

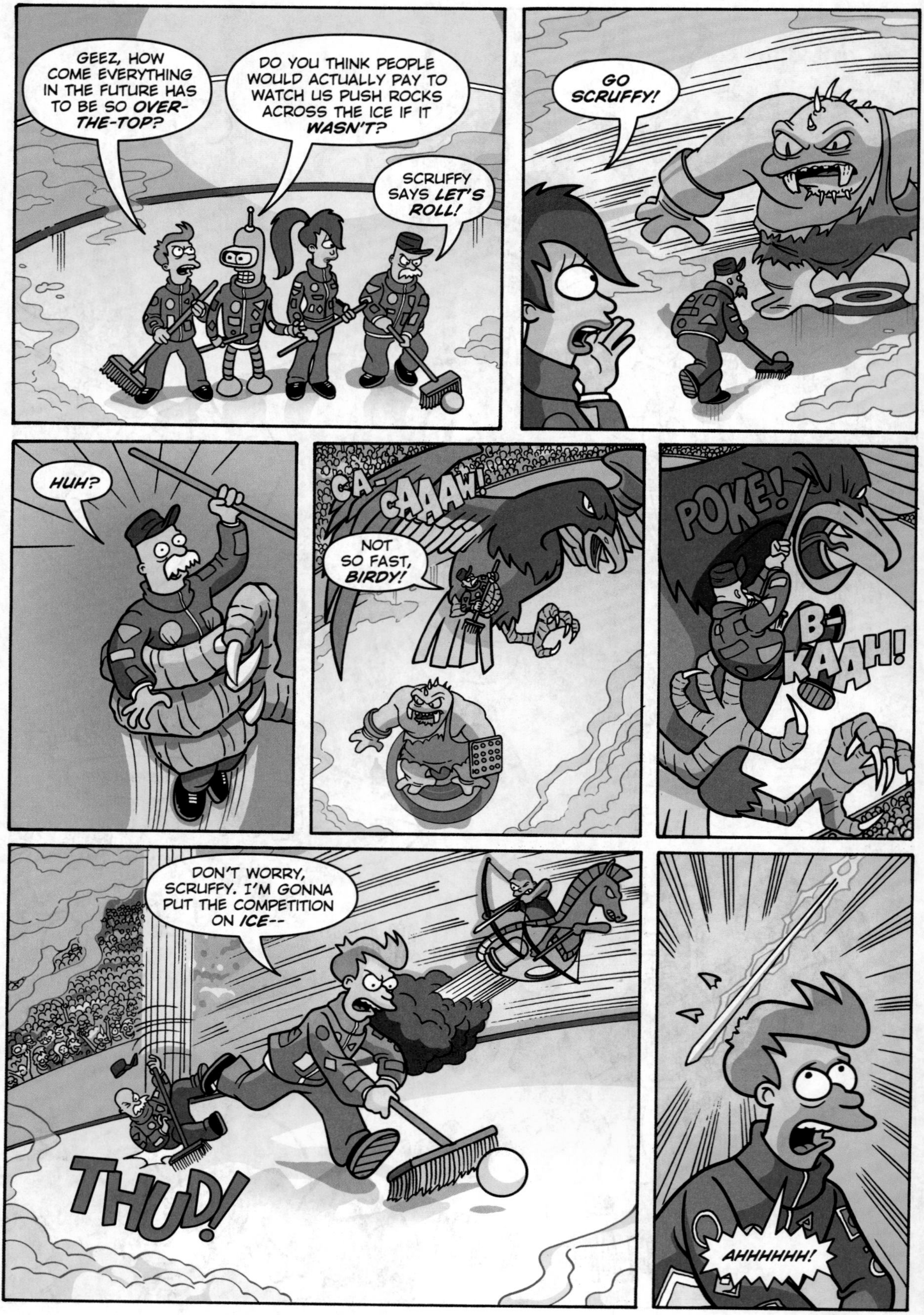
GEEZ, HOW COME EVERYTHING IN THE FUTURE HAS TO BE SO OVER-THE-TOP?
DO YOU THINK PEOPLE WOULD ACTUALLY PAY TO WATCH US PUSH ROCKS ACROSS THE ICE IF IT WASN'T?
SCRUFFY SAYS LET'S ROLL!
GO SCRUFFY!
HUH?
CA-CAAAW!
NOT SO FAST, BIRDY!
POKE!
B-KAAH!
DON'T WORRY, SCRUFFY. I'M GONNA PUT THE COMPETITION ON ICE--
THUD!
AHHHHHH!

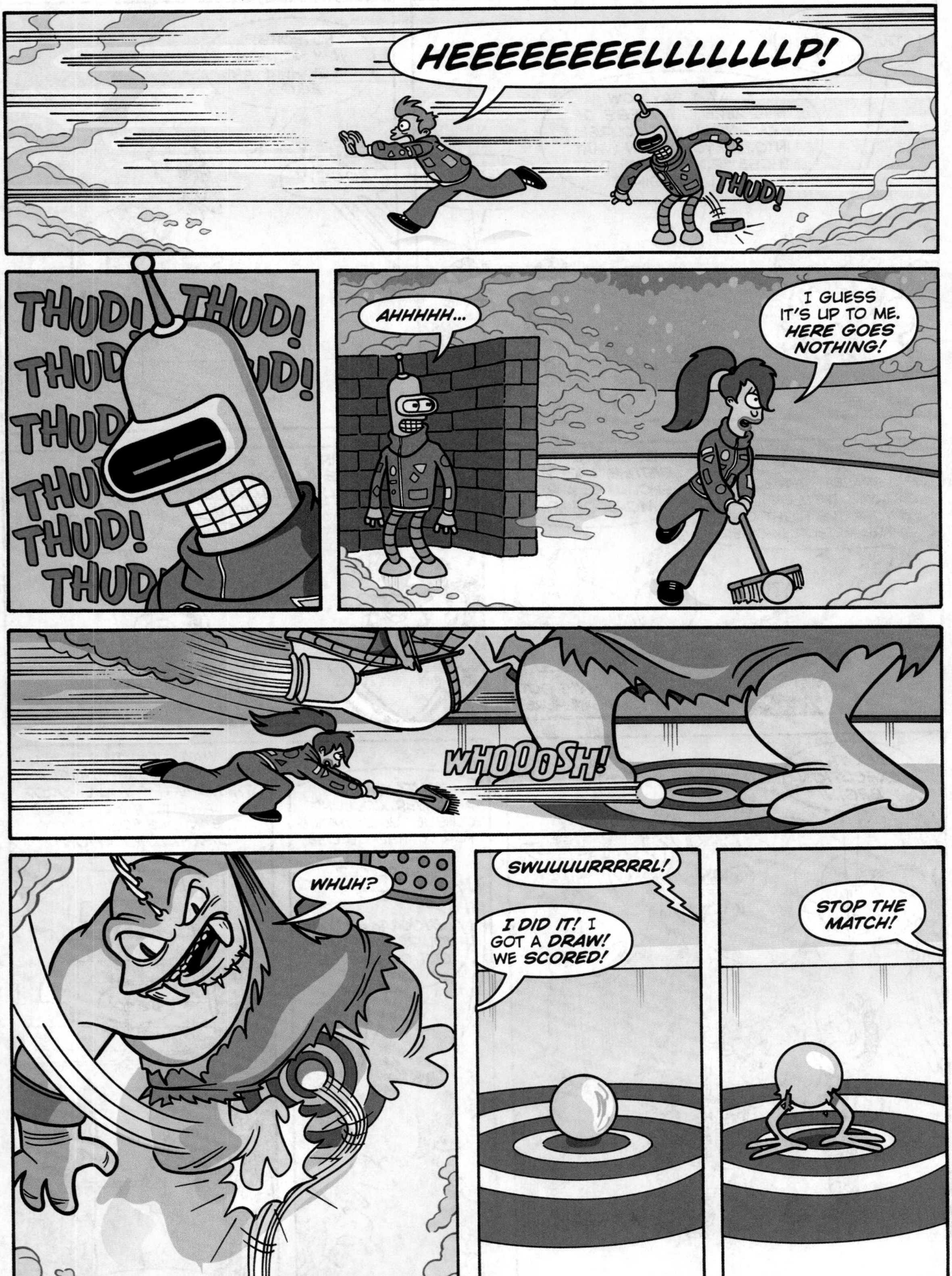

HEEEEEEEELLLLLLLP!
THUD!
THUD! THUD! THUD! THUD! THUD! THUD! THUD!
AHHHHH...
I GUESS IT'S UP TO ME. HERE GOES NOTHING!
WHOOOSH!
WHUH?
SWUUUURRRRRL!
I DID IT! I GOT A DRAW! WE SCORED!
STOP THE MATCH!

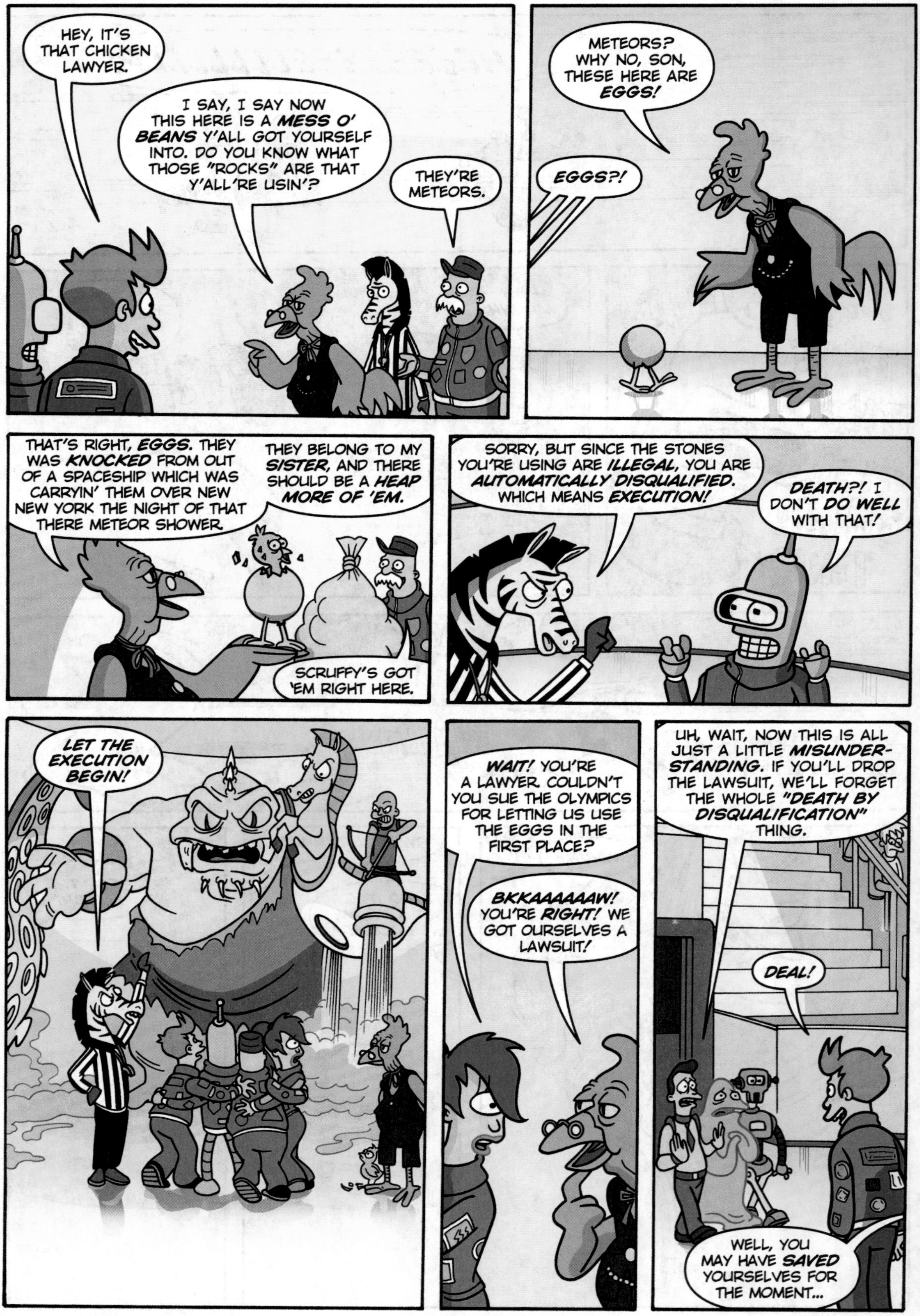
HEY, IT'S THAT CHICKEN LAWYER.
I SAY, I SAY NOW THIS HERE IS A MESS O' BEANS Y'ALL GOT YOURSELF INTO. DO YOU KNOW WHAT THOSE "ROCKS" ARE THAT Y'ALL'RE USIN'?
THEY'RE METEORS.
METEORS? WHY NO, SON, THESE HERE ARE EGGS!
EGGS?!
THAT'S RIGHT, EGGS. THEY WAS KNOCKED FROM OUT OF A SPACESHIP WHICH WAS CARRYIN' THEM OVER NEW NEW YORK THE NIGHT OF THAT THERE METEOR SHOWER.
THEY BELONG TO MY SISTER, AND THERE SHOULD BE A HEAP MORE OF 'EM.
SCRUFFY'S GOT 'EM RIGHT HERE.
SORRY, BUT SINCE THE STONES YOU'RE USING ARE ILLEGAL, YOU ARE AUTOMATICALLY DISQUALIFIED. WHICH MEANS EXECUTION!
DEATH?! I DON'T DO WELL WITH THAT!
LET THE EXECUTION BEGIN!
WAIT! YOU'RE A LAWYER. COULDN'T YOU SUE THE OLYMPICS FOR LETTING US USE THE EGGS IN THE FIRST PLACE?
BKKAAAAAAAW! YOU'RE RIGHT! WE GOT OURSELVES A LAWSUIT!
UH, WAIT, NOW THIS IS ALL JUST A LITTLE MISUNDER-STANDING. IF YOU'LL DROP THE LAWSUIT, WE'LL FORGET THE WHOLE "DEATH BY DISQUALIFICATION" THING.
DEAL!
WELL, YOU MAY HAVE SAVED YOURSELVES FOR THE MOMENT...

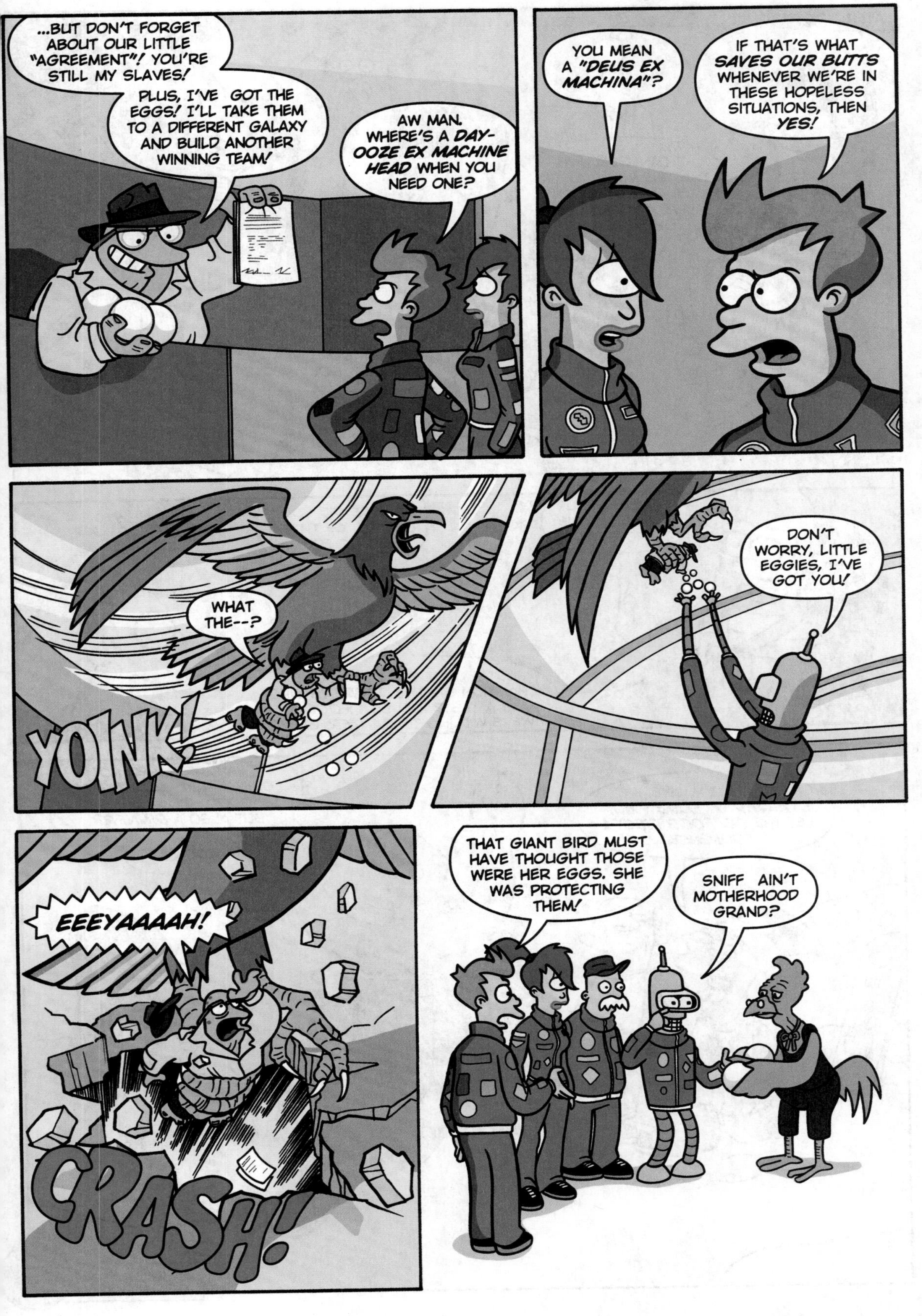
...BUT DON'T FORGET ABOUT OUR LITTLE "AGREEMENT"! YOU'RE STILL MY SLAVES!
PLUS, I'VE GOT THE EGGS! I'LL TAKE THEM TO A DIFFERENT GALAXY AND BUILD ANOTHER WINNING TEAM!
AW MAN. WHERE'S A DAY-OOZE EX MACHINE HEAD WHEN YOU NEED ONE?
YOU MEAN A "DEUS EX MACHINA"?
IF THAT'S WHAT SAVES OUR BUTTS WHENEVER WE'RE IN THESE HOPELESS SITUATIONS, THEN YES!
WHAT THE--?
YOINK!
DON'T WORRY, LITTLE EGGIES, I'VE GOT YOU!
EEEYAAAAH!
CRASH!
THAT GIANT BIRD MUST HAVE THOUGHT THOSE WERE HER EGGS. SHE WAS PROTECTING THEM!
SNIFF AIN'T MOTHERHOOD GRAND?

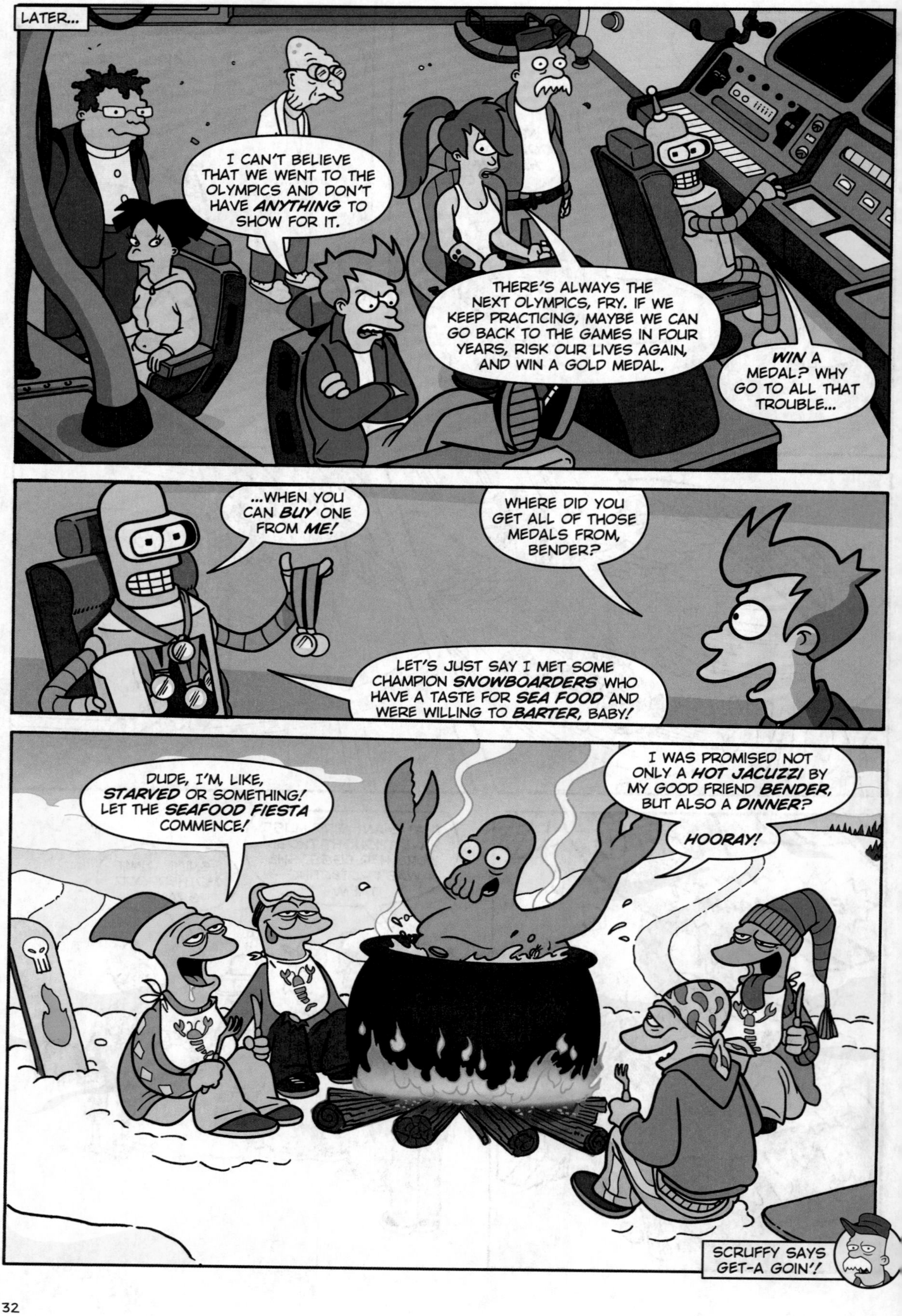

LATER...
I CAN'T BELIEVE THAT WE WENT TO THE OLYMPICS AND DON'T HAVE *ANYTHING* TO SHOW FOR IT.
THERE'S ALWAYS THE NEXT OLYMPICS, FRY. IF WE KEEP PRACTICING, MAYBE WE CAN GO BACK TO THE GAMES IN FOUR YEARS, RISK OUR LIVES AGAIN, AND WIN A GOLD MEDAL.
WIN A MEDAL? WHY GO TO ALL THAT TROUBLE...
...WHEN YOU CAN *BUY* ONE FROM *ME!*
WHERE DID YOU GET ALL OF THOSE MEDALS FROM, BENDER?
LET'S JUST SAY I MET SOME CHAMPION *SNOWBOARDERS* WHO HAVE A TASTE FOR *SEA FOOD* AND WERE WILLING TO *BARTER*, BABY!
DUDE, I'M, LIKE, *STARVED* OR SOMETHING! LET THE *SEAFOOD FIESTA* COMMENCE!
I WAS PROMISED NOT ONLY A *HOT JACUZZI* BY MY GOOD FRIEND *BENDER*, BUT ALSO A *DINNER?*
HOORAY!
SCRUFFY SAYS GET-A GOIN'!

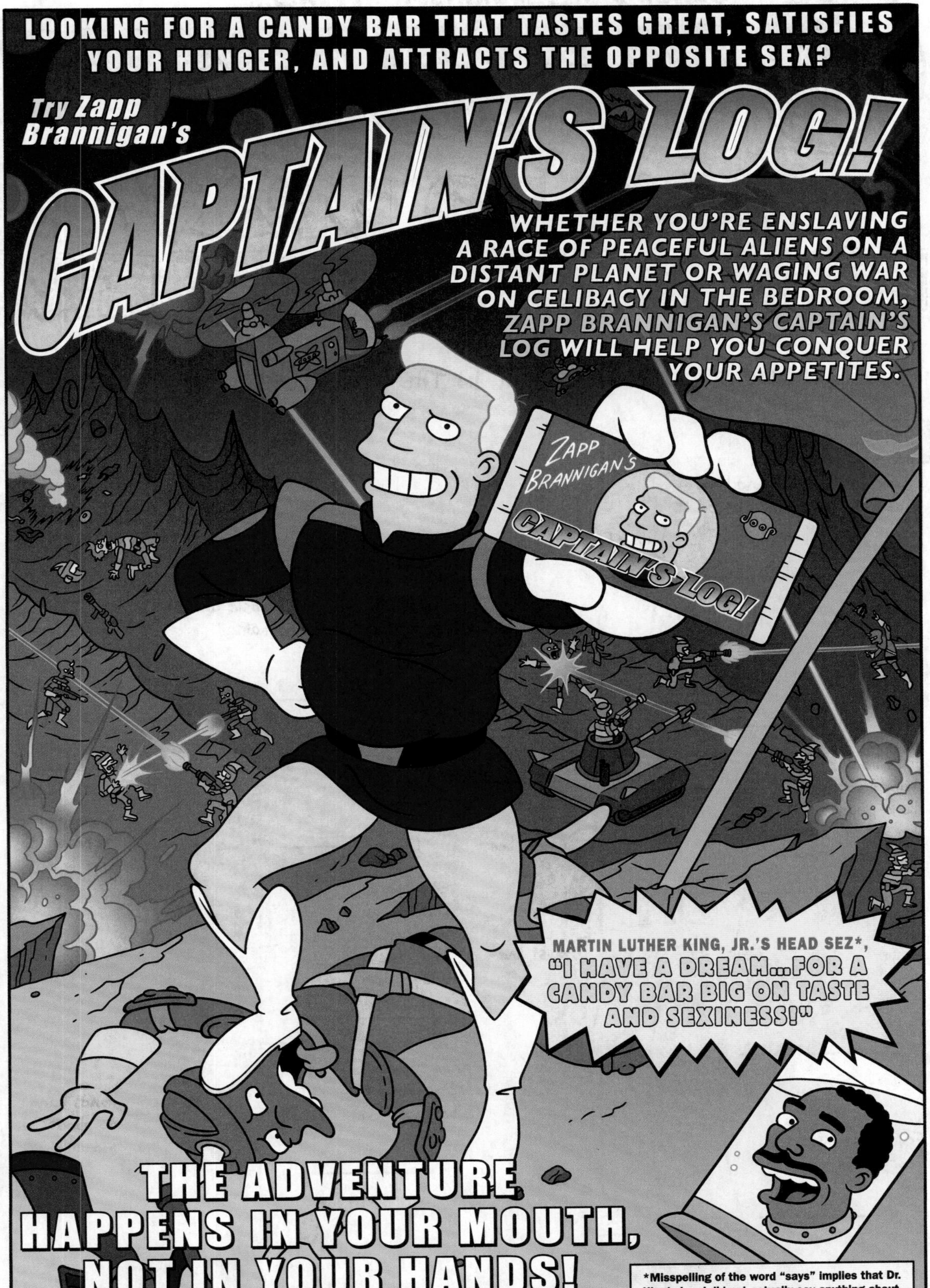
LOOKING FOR A CANDY BAR THAT TASTES GREAT, SATISFIES YOUR HUNGER, AND ATTRACTS THE OPPOSITE SEX?
Try Zapp Brannigan's
CAPTAIN'S LOG!
WHETHER YOU'RE ENSLAVING A RACE OF PEACEFUL ALIENS ON A DISTANT PLANET OR WAGING WAR ON CELIBACY IN THE BEDROOM, ZAPP BRANNIGAN'S CAPTAIN'S LOG WILL HELP YOU CONQUER YOUR APPETITES.
ZAPP BRANNIGAN'S
CAPTAIN'S LOG!
MARTIN LUTHER KING, JR.'S HEAD SEZ*,
"I HAVE A DREAM...FOR A CANDY BAR BIG ON TASTE AND SEXINESS!"
THE ADVENTURE HAPPENS IN YOUR MOUTH, NOT IN YOUR HANDS!
Sold at fine 7-11 stores across the universe.
*Misspelling of the word "says" implies that Dr. King's head did not actually say anything about Zapp Brannigan's Captain's Log candy bar.

BONGO'S BILL MORRISON REVEALS...

THE CLOSELY-GUARDED SECRETS OF

HOW TO DRAW FRY AND BENDER!

SINCE WE MENTIONED FRY FIRST IN THE TITLE, LET'S START WITH HIM!

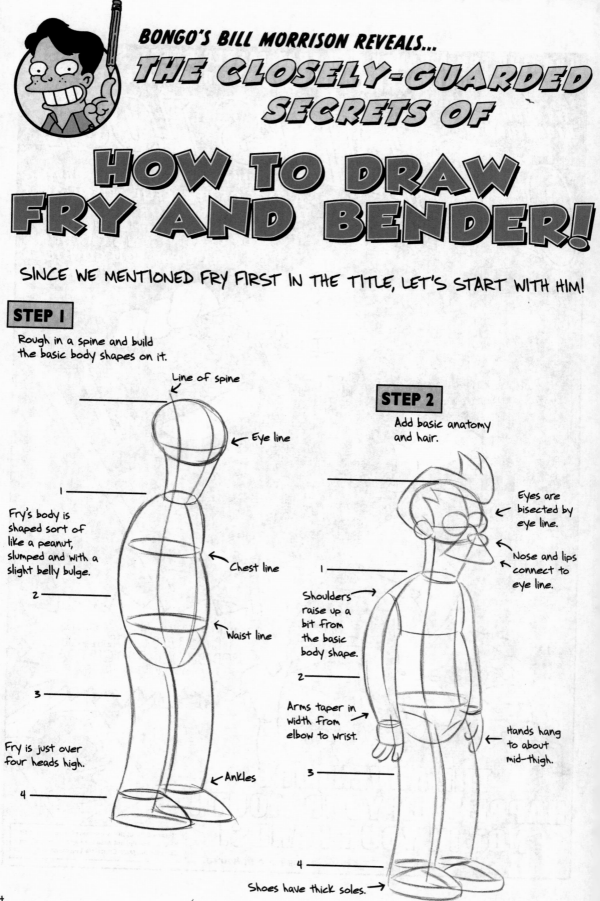

STEP 1

Rough in a spine and build the basic body shapes on it.

Line of spine

Eye line

1

Fry's body is shaped sort of like a peanut, slumped and with a slight belly bulge.

2

Chest line

Waist line

3

Fry is just over four heads high.

4

Ankles

STEP 2

Add basic anatomy and hair.

Eyes are bisected by eye line.

Nose and lips connect to eye line.

1

Shoulders raise up a bit from the basic body shape.

2

Arms taper in width from elbow to wrist.

Hands hang to about mid-thigh.

3

4

Shoes have thick soles.

STEP 3

Add clothing and details.

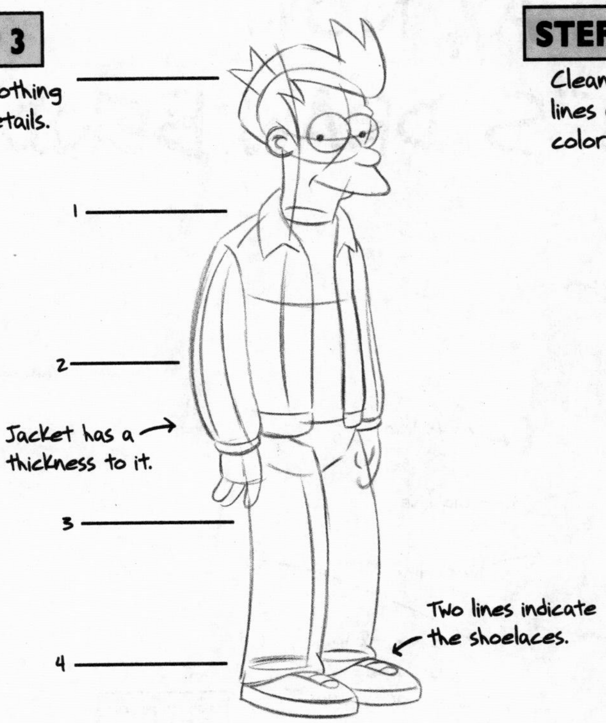
1
2
3
4
Jacket has a thickness to it.
Two lines indicate the shoelaces.

STEP 4

Clean up your lines and add color.

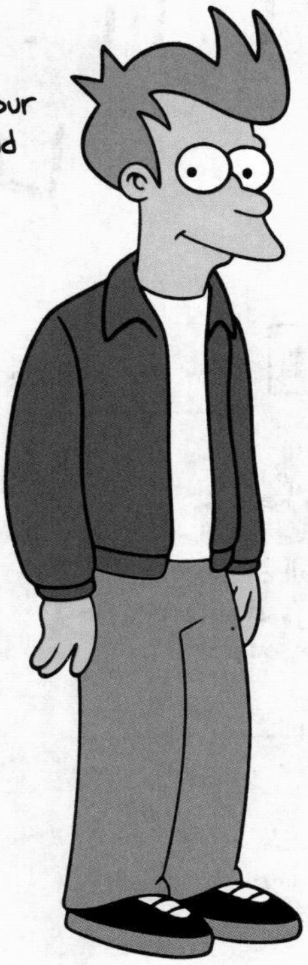

NOW LET'S TAKE A CLOSER LOOK AT FRY'S HEAD!

STEP 1

Start with an oval for the skull. Then draw the neck dropping from the front of the skull.

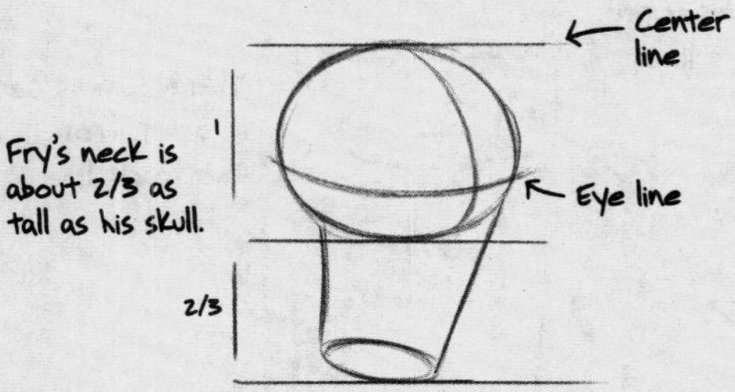
Center line
Eye line
Fry's neck is about 2/3 as tall as his skull.
1
2/3

STEP 2

Add facial features and hair.

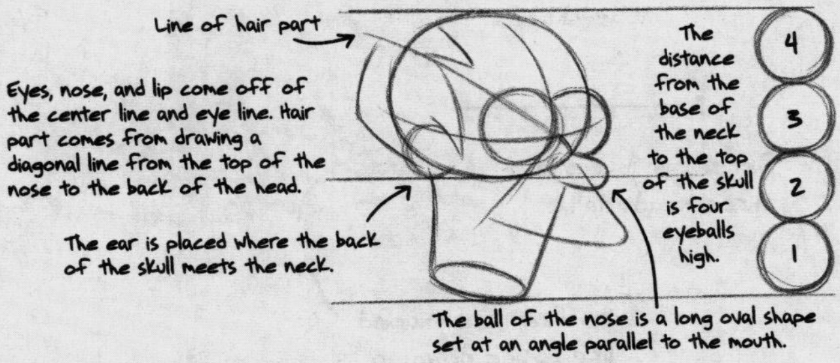
Line of hair part
Eyes, nose, and lip come off of the center line and eye line. Hair part comes from drawing a diagonal line from the top of the nose to the back of the head.
The ear is placed where the back of the skull meets the neck.
The distance from the base of the neck to the top of the skull is four eyeballs high.
4
3
2
1
The ball of the nose is a long oval shape set at an angle parallel to the mouth.

STEP 3

Finish the rest of the hair.

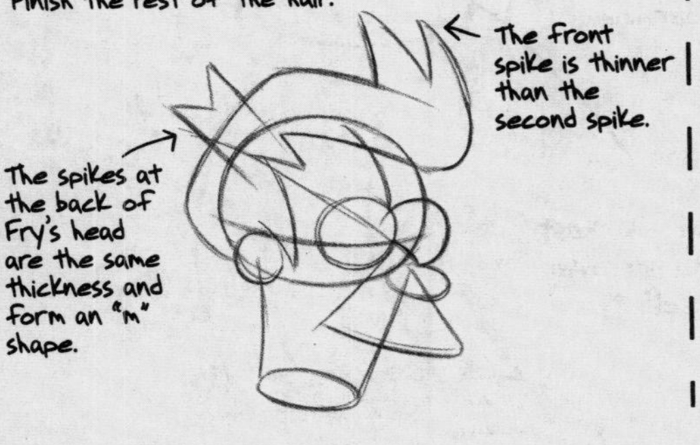
The front spike is thinner than the second spike.
The spikes at the back of Fry's head are the same thickness and form an "m" shape.

STEP 4

Add details.

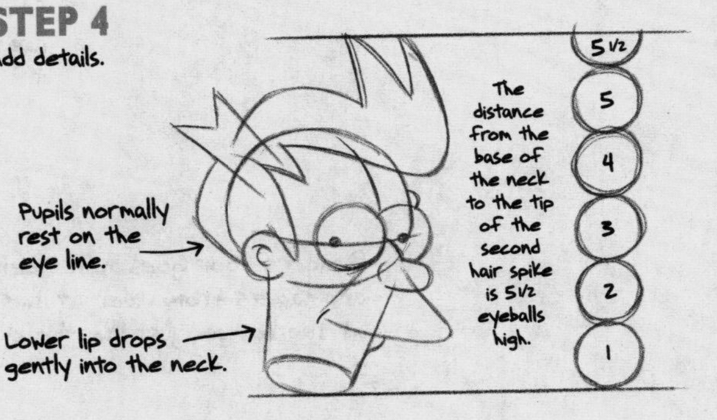
Pupils normally rest on the eye line.
Lower lip drops gently into the neck.
The distance from the base of the neck to the tip of the second hair spike is 5½ eyeballs high.
5½
5
4
3
2
1

GOT IT? OKAY, NOW LET'S DRAW BENDER!

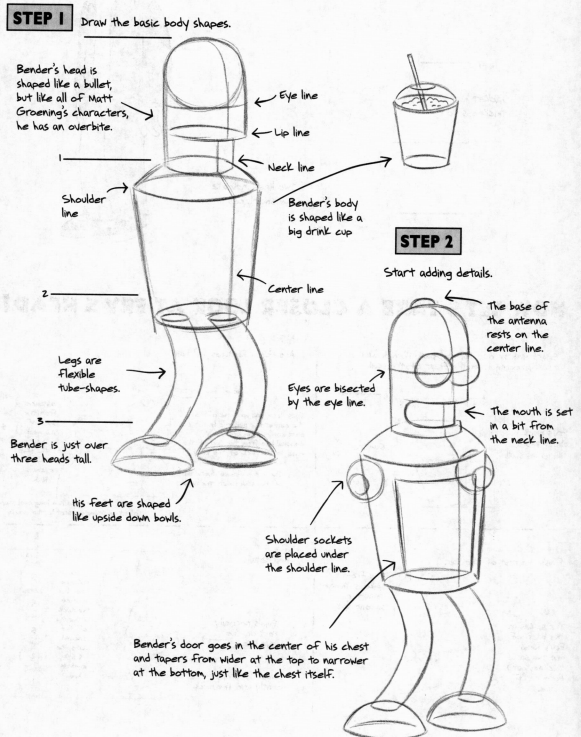

STEP 1 Draw the basic body shapes.

Bender's head is shaped like a bullet, but like all of Matt Groening's characters, he has an overbite.

← Eye line

← Lip line

← Neck line

1 —————

Shoulder line

Bender's body is shaped like a big drink cup

← Center line

STEP 2

Start adding details.

← The base of the antenna rests on the center line.

Eyes are bisected by the eye line.

← The mouth is set in a bit from the neck line.

2 —————

Legs are flexible tube-shapes.

3 —————

Bender is just over three heads tall.

Shoulder sockets are placed under the shoulder line.

His feet are shaped like upside down bowls.

Bender's door goes in the center of his chest and tapers from wider at the top to narrower at the bottom, just like the chest itself.

STEP 4

Finish adding details.

Bender's antenna is a tapered tube with a ball on top. It rises straight up from the base.

Pupils are square and normally rest on the eye line.

His eye expression changes by using black eye lid shapes.

Add two curved horizontal lines to complete Bender's "teeth".

Place the round doorknob on the right side of the door, half way between the top and bottom of the door.

Add five segment lines to each arm (including the elbow line).

Round off the corners of the door.

Add five segment lines to each leg (including the knee line).

STEP 3

Add more details.

Lay the visor over the eyes so they are completely encased inside.

The back of the visor should line up with the back of the mouth.

Draw vertical lines at equal distance from each other for Bender's "teeth".

Bender's arms are flexible tube shapes, slightly more narrow than his legs.

Draw the elbow line halfway between his hand and shoulder.

Draw the knee line halfway between his foot and body.

The hands hang down to just above the knees.

STEP 5

Clean up your lines and add color.

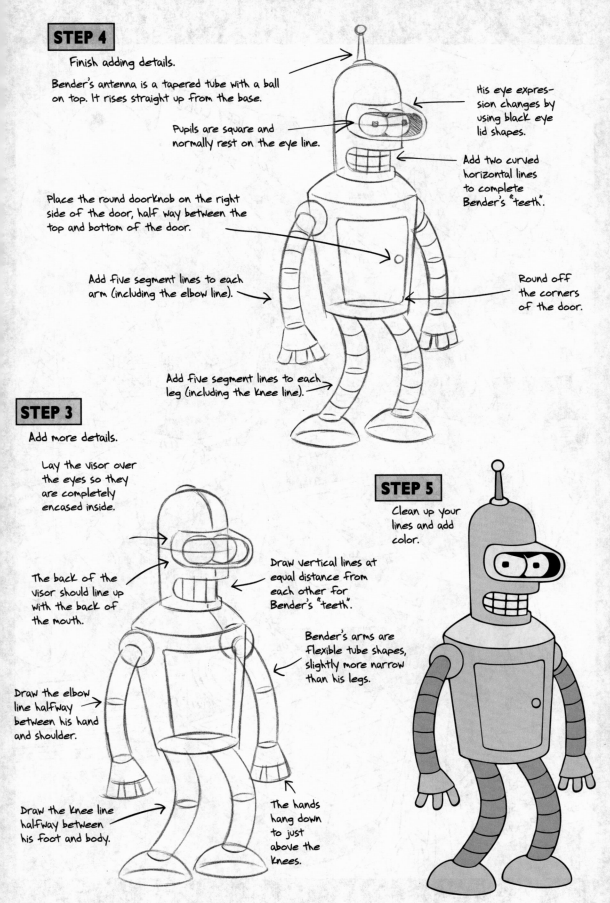

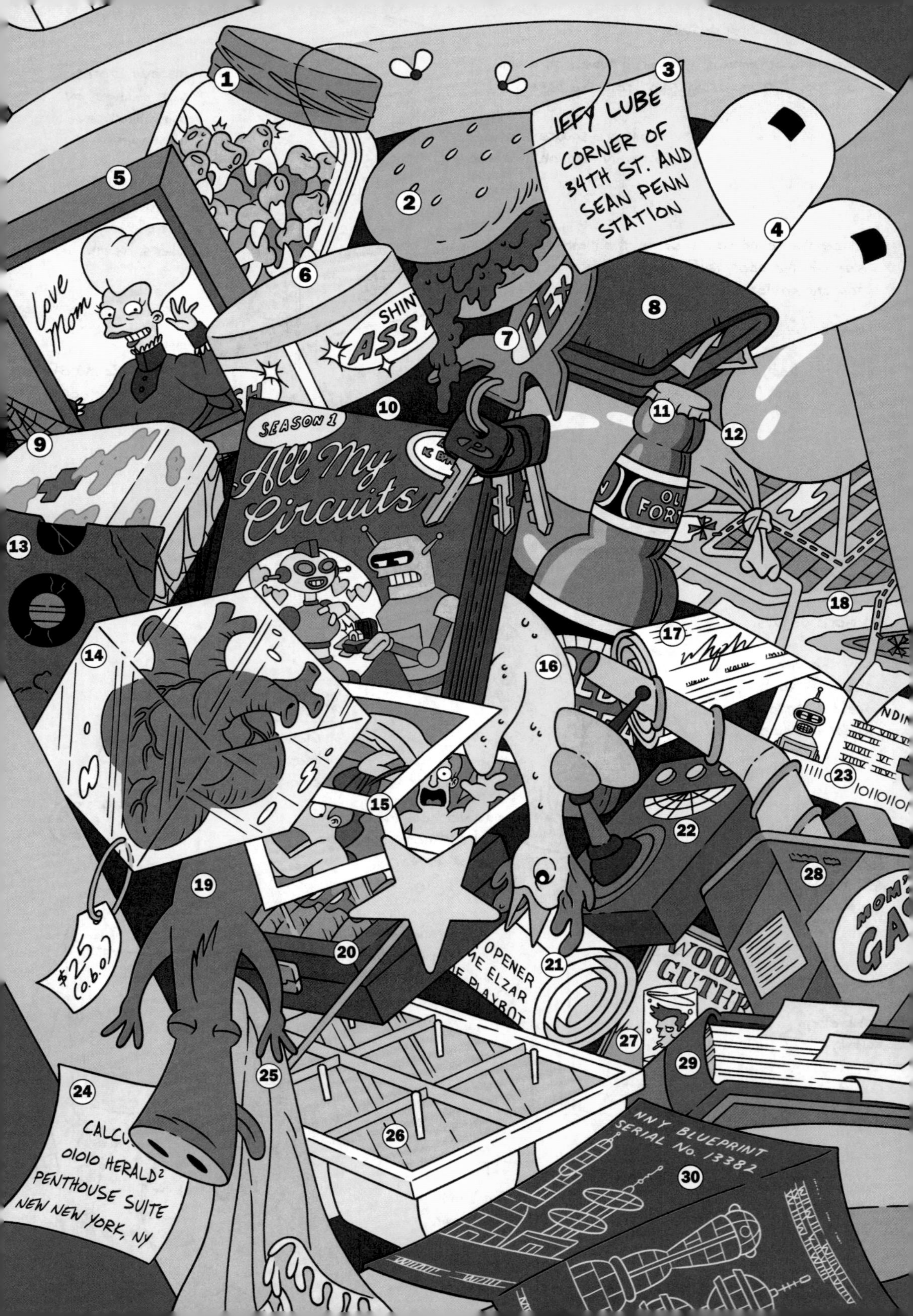
1
2
3
IEFY LUBE
CORNER OF
34TH ST. AND
SEAN PENN
STATION
4
5
Love Mom
6
SHINY
ASS
7
8
9
10
SEASON 1
All My Circuits
11
12
13
14
15
16
17
18
19
$25 (o.b.o.)
20
21
OPENER
22
23
24
CALCU
01010 HERALD²
PENTHOUSE SUITE
NEW NEW YORK, NY
25
26
27
28
29
NNY BLUEPRINT
SERIAL No. 13382
30

Let's see... WHAT'S IN BENDER'S CHEST!

1. Collection of Gold Teeth from Grave-Robbed Corpses
2. Hermes' Manwich
3. Calculon's Favorite Oil Change Shop
4. Extra Pair of Eyes
5. Photo of MOM
6. Shiny Metal Brand® Ass Polish
7. Duplicate Set of Keys to Planet Express Ship
8. Fry's Wallet
9. First Aid Kit (never been used)
10. "All My Circuits: Season One" DVD set
11. Beer
12. Water Balloons Filled with Slurm™
13. Little Black Disk (with phone numbers of loose fembots)
14. Some Guy's Heart
15. Compromising Photos of Fry
16. Rubber Chicken
17. Restraining Order to Stay Away from Calculon
18. Calculon's Path from Home to Work
19. Forgotten Spice Weasel (dead)
20. Cigar Humidor
21. X-mas List for Robot Santa
22. Gay-dar Satellite Controls
23. Bending License
24. Calculon's Address
25. "Gender Bender" Tu-tu and Wand
26. Booz-cicles
27. Professor's Folk Music CD (Woody Guthrie's Head Live at Headstock)
28. Gasoline Can
29. Elzar's Personal Cookbook
30. Blueprint Diagram of Bank Of New New York

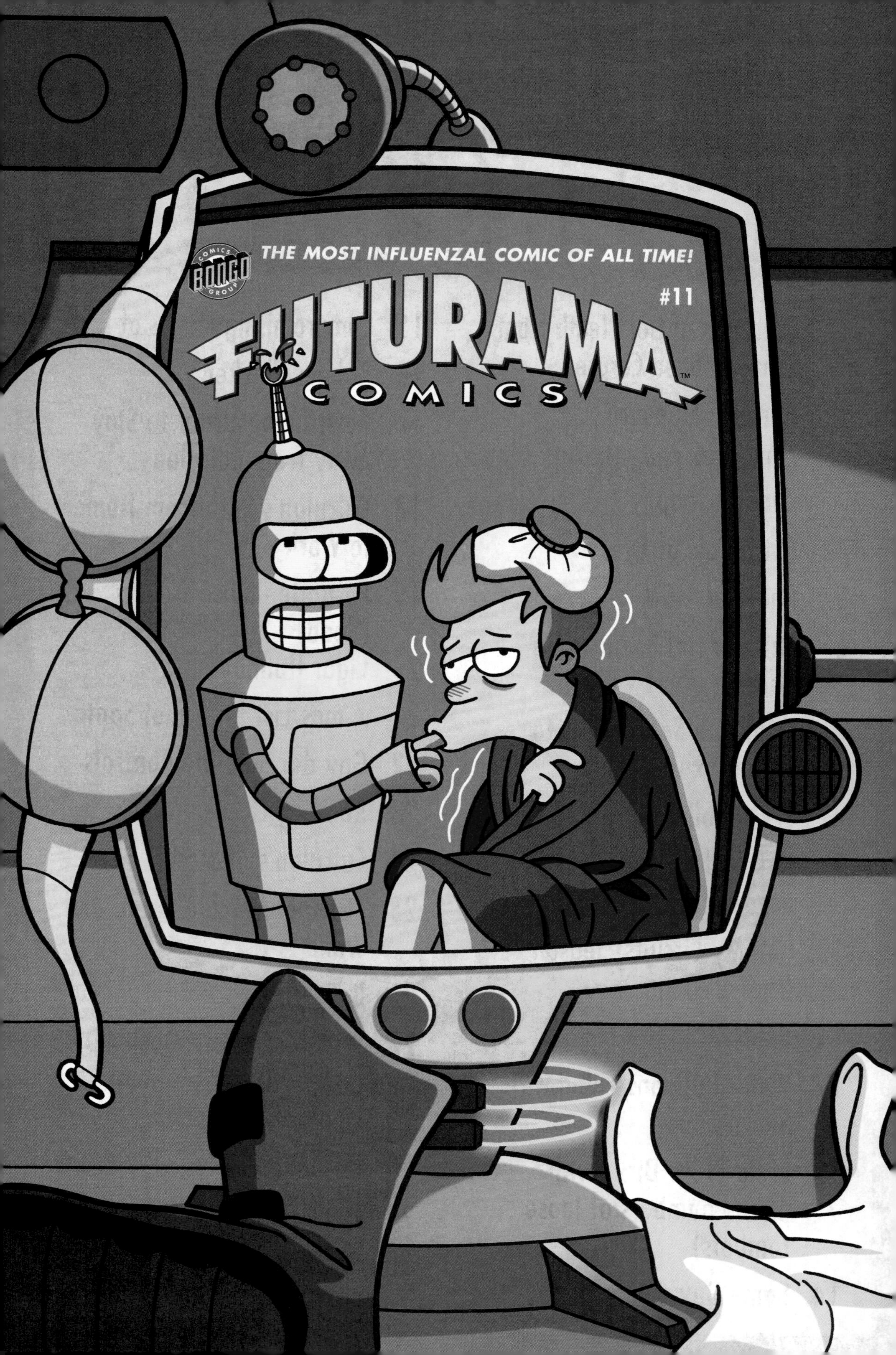

THE MOST INFLUENZAL COMIC OF ALL TIME!
#11
FUTURAMA COMICS

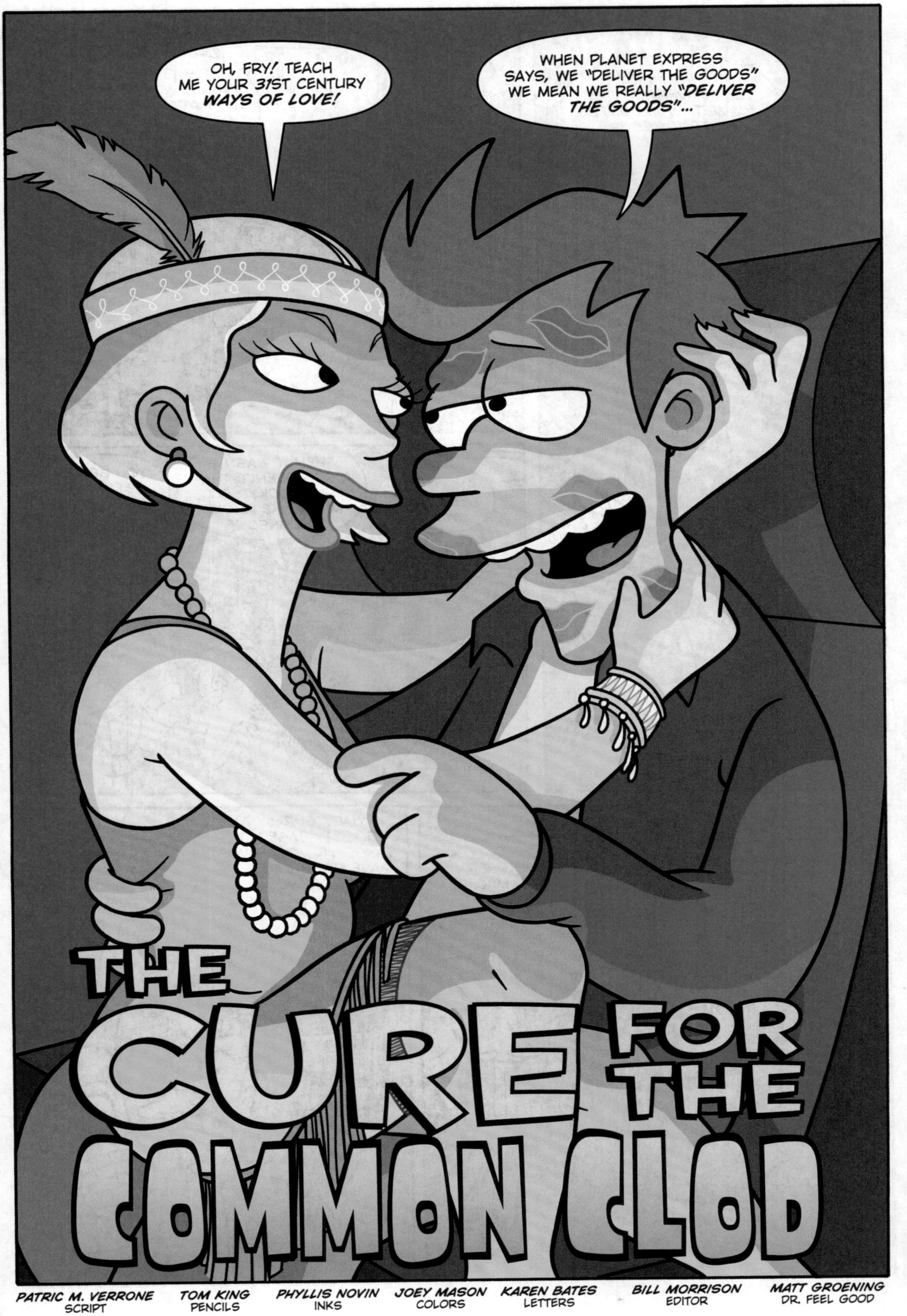
OH, FRY! TEACH ME YOUR 31ST CENTURY WAYS OF LOVE!
WHEN PLANET EXPRESS SAYS, WE "DELIVER THE GOODS" WE MEAN WE REALLY "DELIVER THE GOODS"...
THE CURE FOR THE COMMON CLOD

PATRIC M. VERRONE SCRIPT · TOM KING PENCILS · PHYLLIS NOVIN INKS · JOEY MASON COLORS · KAREN BATES LETTERS · BILL MORRISON EDITOR · MATT GROENING DR. FEEL GOOD

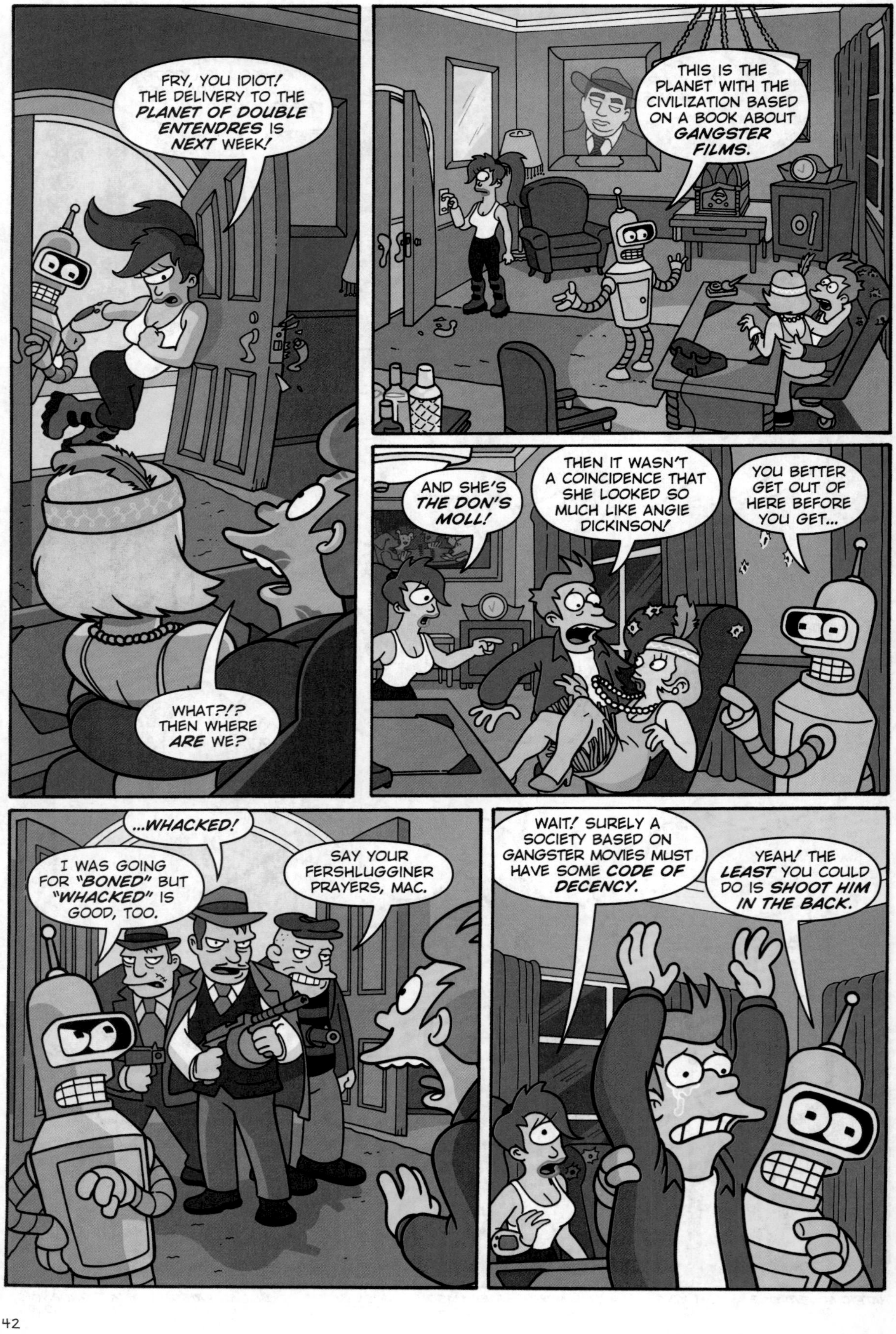
FRY, YOU IDIOT! THE DELIVERY TO THE PLANET OF DOUBLE ENTENDRES IS NEXT WEEK!
WHAT?!? THEN WHERE ARE WE?
THIS IS THE PLANET WITH THE CIVILIZATION BASED ON A BOOK ABOUT GANGSTER FILMS.
AND SHE'S THE DON'S MOLL!
THEN IT WASN'T A COINCIDENCE THAT SHE LOOKED SO MUCH LIKE ANGIE DICKINSON!
YOU BETTER GET OUT OF HERE BEFORE YOU GET...
...WHACKED!
I WAS GOING FOR "BONED" BUT "WHACKED" IS GOOD, TOO.
SAY YOUR FERSHLUGGINER PRAYERS, MAC.
WAIT! SURELY A SOCIETY BASED ON GANGSTER MOVIES MUST HAVE SOME CODE OF DECENCY.
YEAH! THE LEAST YOU COULD DO IS SHOOT HIM IN THE BACK.

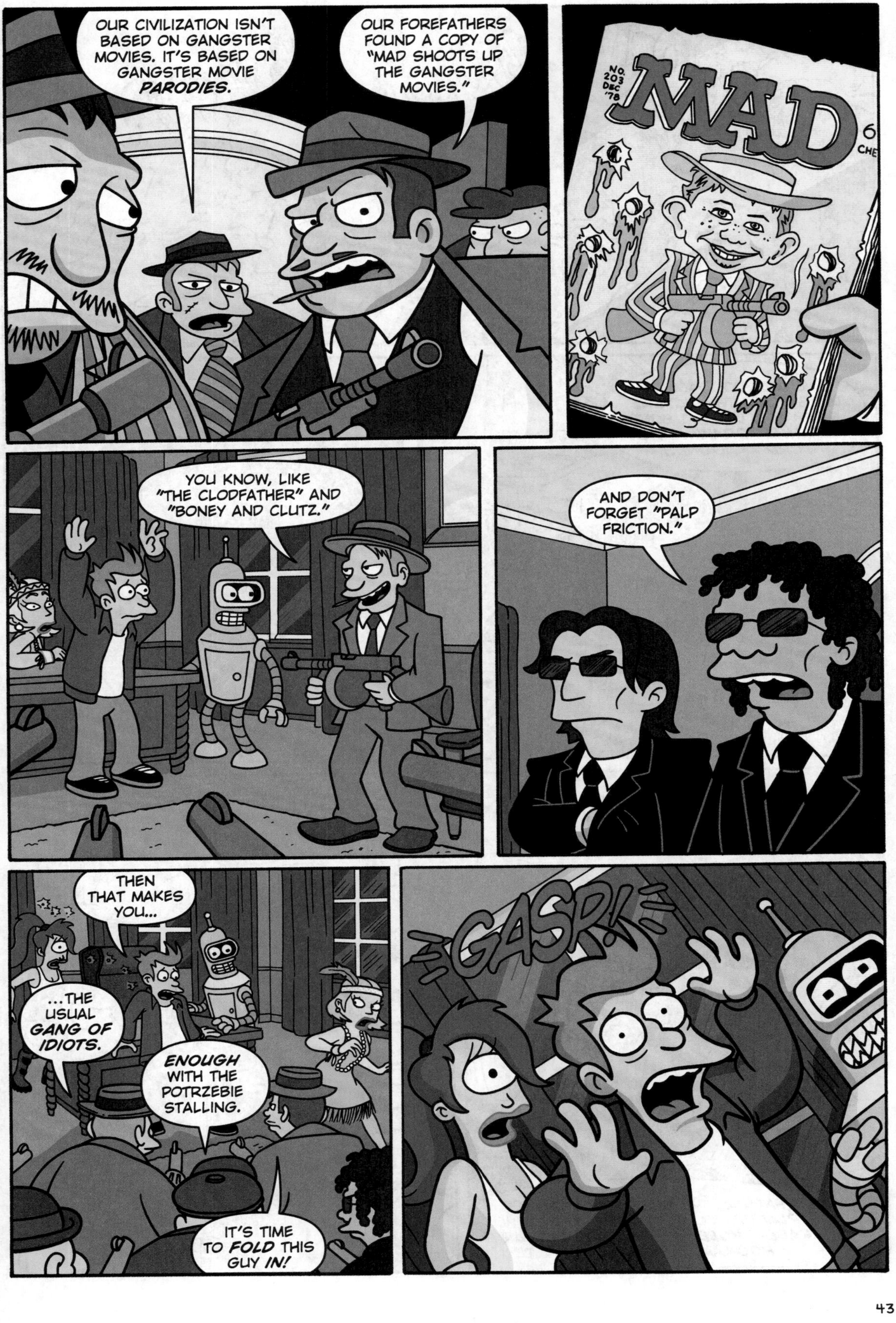
OUR CIVILIZATION ISN'T BASED ON GANGSTER MOVIES. IT'S BASED ON GANGSTER MOVIE *PARODIES.*
OUR FOREFATHERS FOUND A COPY OF "MAD SHOOTS UP THE GANGSTER MOVIES."
NO. 203 DEC '78
MAD
YOU KNOW, LIKE "THE CLODFATHER" AND "BONEY AND CLUTZ."
AND DON'T FORGET "PALP FRICTION."
THEN THAT MAKES YOU...
...THE USUAL *GANG OF IDIOTS.*
ENOUGH WITH THE POTRZEBIE STALLING.
IT'S TIME TO *FOLD* THIS GUY *IN!*
GASP!

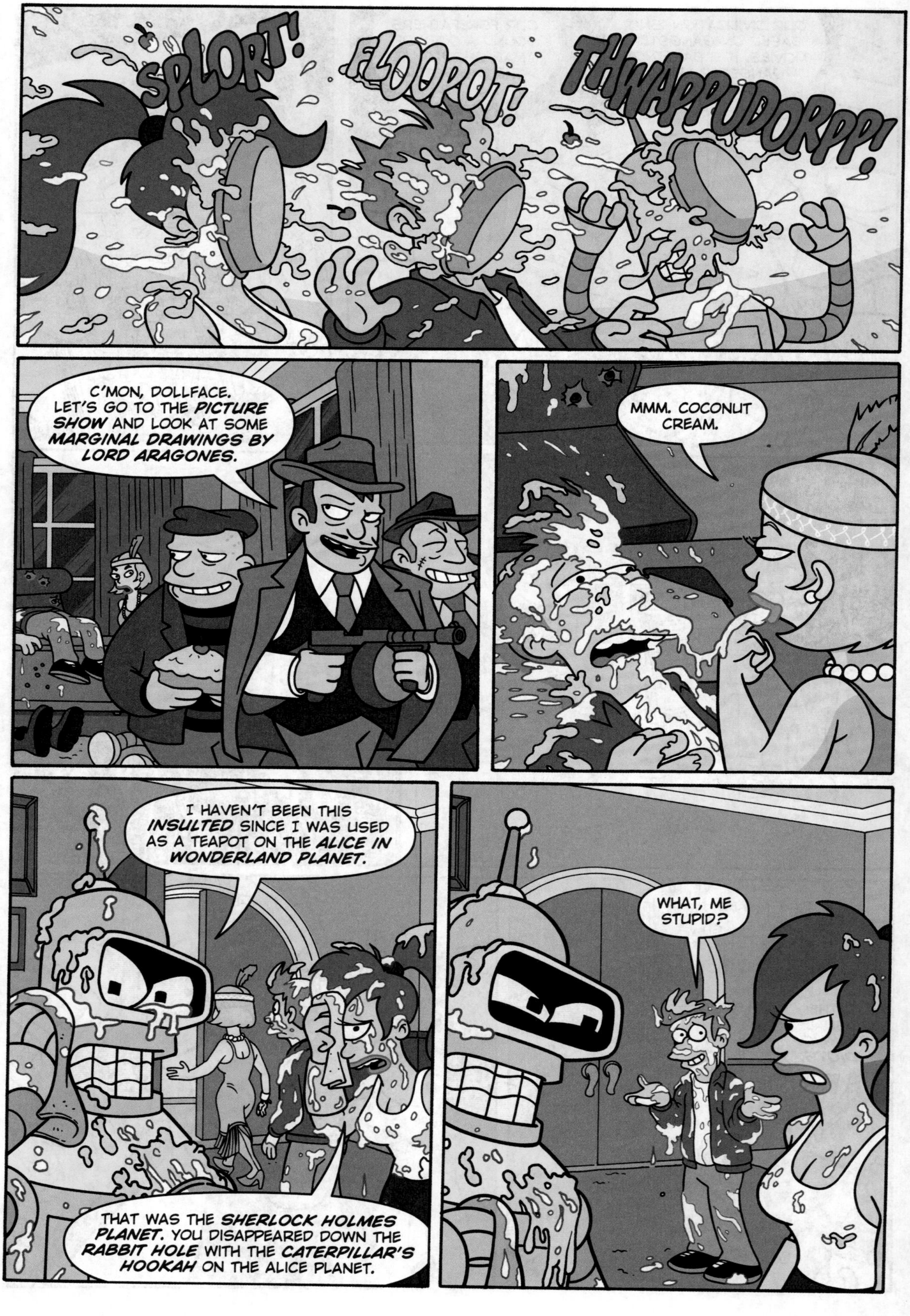

SPLORT!
FLOOPOT!
THWAPPUDORPP!
C'MON, DOLLFACE. LET'S GO TO THE PICTURE SHOW AND LOOK AT SOME MARGINAL DRAWINGS BY LORD ARAGONES.
MMM. COCONUT CREAM.
I HAVEN'T BEEN THIS INSULTED SINCE I WAS USED AS A TEAPOT ON THE ALICE IN WONDERLAND PLANET.
THAT WAS THE SHERLOCK HOLMES PLANET. YOU DISAPPEARED DOWN THE RABBIT HOLE WITH THE CATERPILLAR'S HOOKAH ON THE ALICE PLANET.
WHAT, ME STUPID?

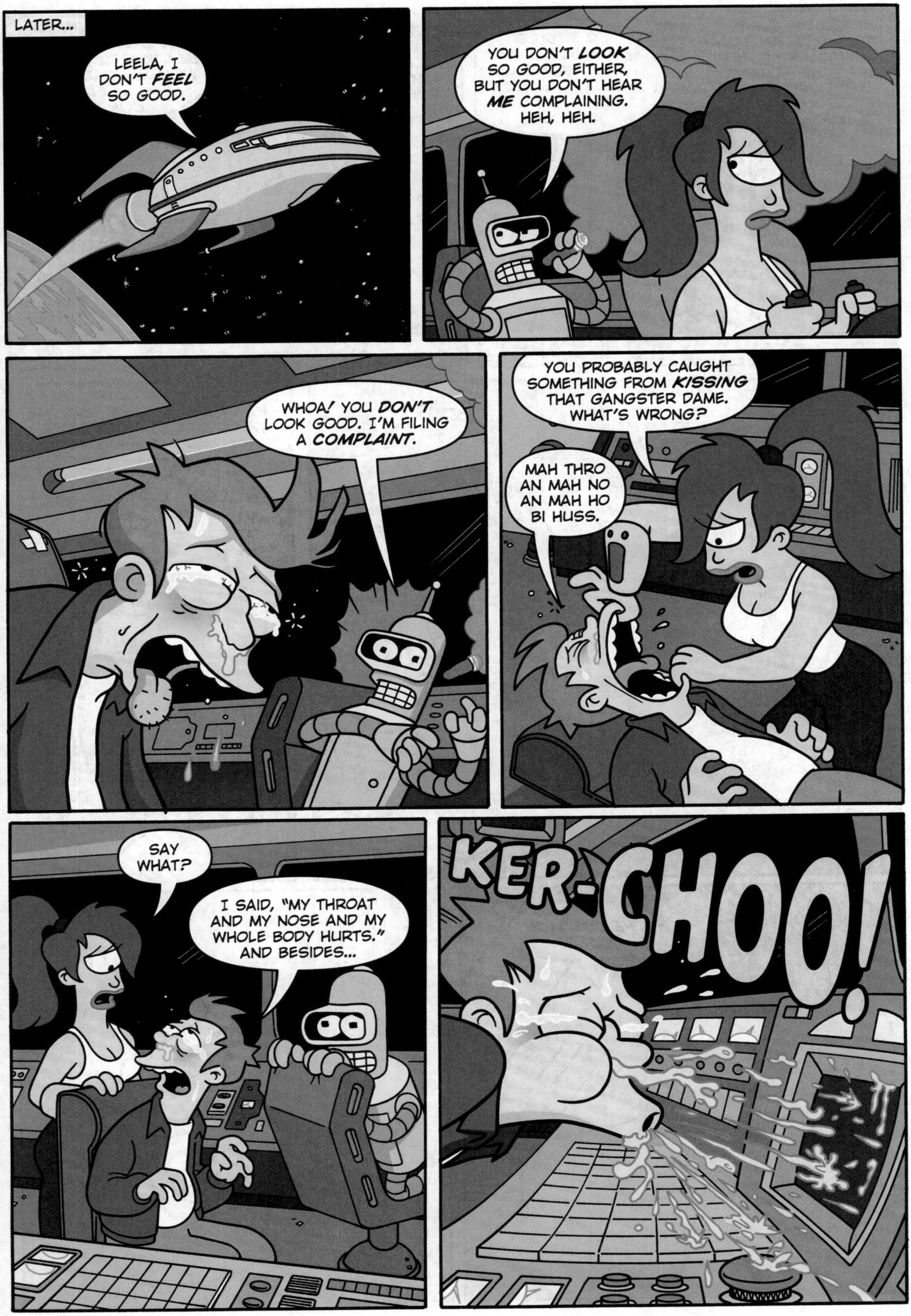
LATER...
LEELA, I DON'T FEEL SO GOOD.
YOU DON'T LOOK SO GOOD, EITHER, BUT YOU DON'T HEAR ME COMPLAINING. HEH, HEH.
WHOA! YOU DON'T LOOK GOOD. I'M FILING A COMPLAINT.
YOU PROBABLY CAUGHT SOMETHING FROM KISSING THAT GANGSTER DAME. WHAT'S WRONG?
MAH THRO AN MAH NO AN MAH HO BI HUSS.
SAY WHAT?
I SAID, "MY THROAT AND MY NOSE AND MY WHOLE BODY HURTS." AND BESIDES...
KER-CHOO!

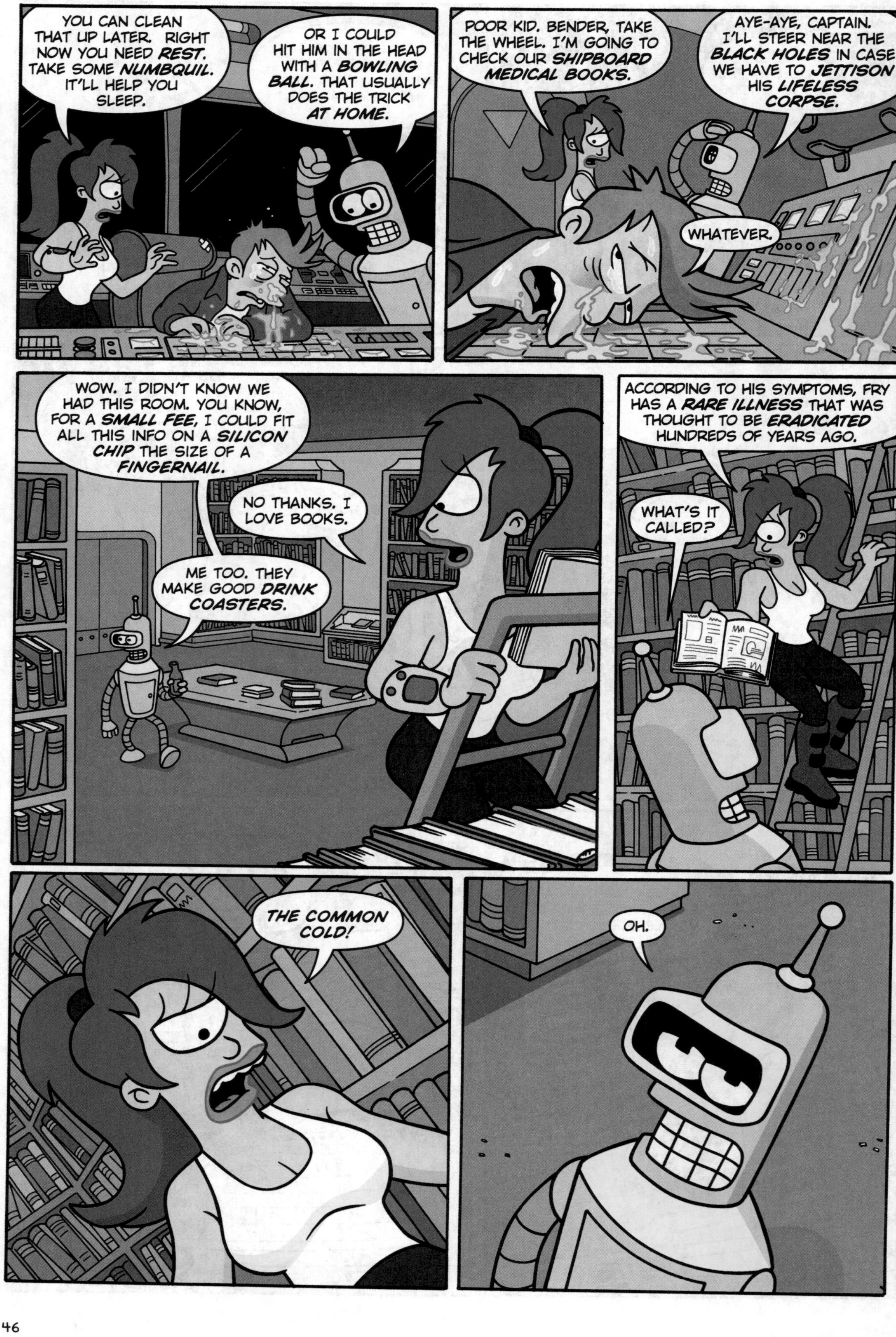
YOU CAN CLEAN THAT UP LATER. RIGHT NOW YOU NEED REST. TAKE SOME NUMBQUIL. IT'LL HELP YOU SLEEP.
OR I COULD HIT HIM IN THE HEAD WITH A BOWLING BALL. THAT USUALLY DOES THE TRICK AT HOME.
POOR KID. BENDER, TAKE THE WHEEL. I'M GOING TO CHECK OUR SHIPBOARD MEDICAL BOOKS.
AYE-AYE, CAPTAIN. I'LL STEER NEAR THE BLACK HOLES IN CASE WE HAVE TO JETTISON HIS LIFELESS CORPSE.
WHATEVER.
WOW. I DIDN'T KNOW WE HAD THIS ROOM. YOU KNOW, FOR A SMALL FEE, I COULD FIT ALL THIS INFO ON A SILICON CHIP THE SIZE OF A FINGERNAIL.
NO THANKS. I LOVE BOOKS.
ME TOO. THEY MAKE GOOD DRINK COASTERS.
ACCORDING TO HIS SYMPTOMS, FRY HAS A RARE ILLNESS THAT WAS THOUGHT TO BE ERADICATED HUNDREDS OF YEARS AGO.
WHAT'S IT CALLED?
THE COMMON COLD!
OH.

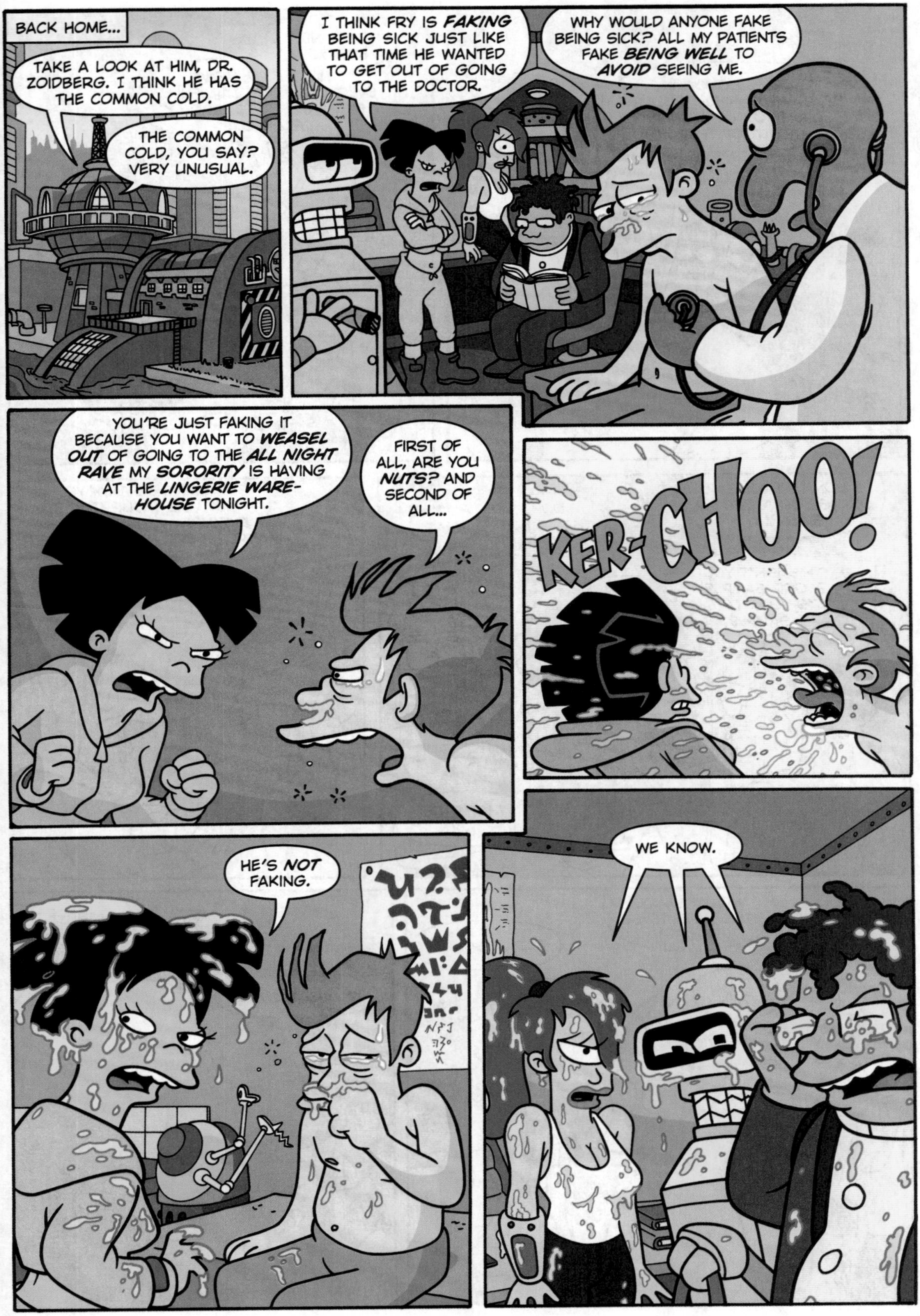

BACK HOME...
TAKE A LOOK AT HIM, DR. ZOIDBERG. I THINK HE HAS THE COMMON COLD.
THE COMMON COLD, YOU SAY? VERY UNUSUAL.
I THINK FRY IS FAKING BEING SICK JUST LIKE THAT TIME HE WANTED TO GET OUT OF GOING TO THE DOCTOR.
WHY WOULD ANYONE FAKE BEING SICK? ALL MY PATIENTS FAKE BEING WELL TO AVOID SEEING ME.
YOU'RE JUST FAKING IT BECAUSE YOU WANT TO WEASEL OUT OF GOING TO THE ALL NIGHT RAVE MY SORORITY IS HAVING AT THE LINGERIE WARE-HOUSE TONIGHT.
FIRST OF ALL, ARE YOU NUTS? AND SECOND OF ALL...
KER-CHOO!
HE'S NOT FAKING.
WE KNOW.

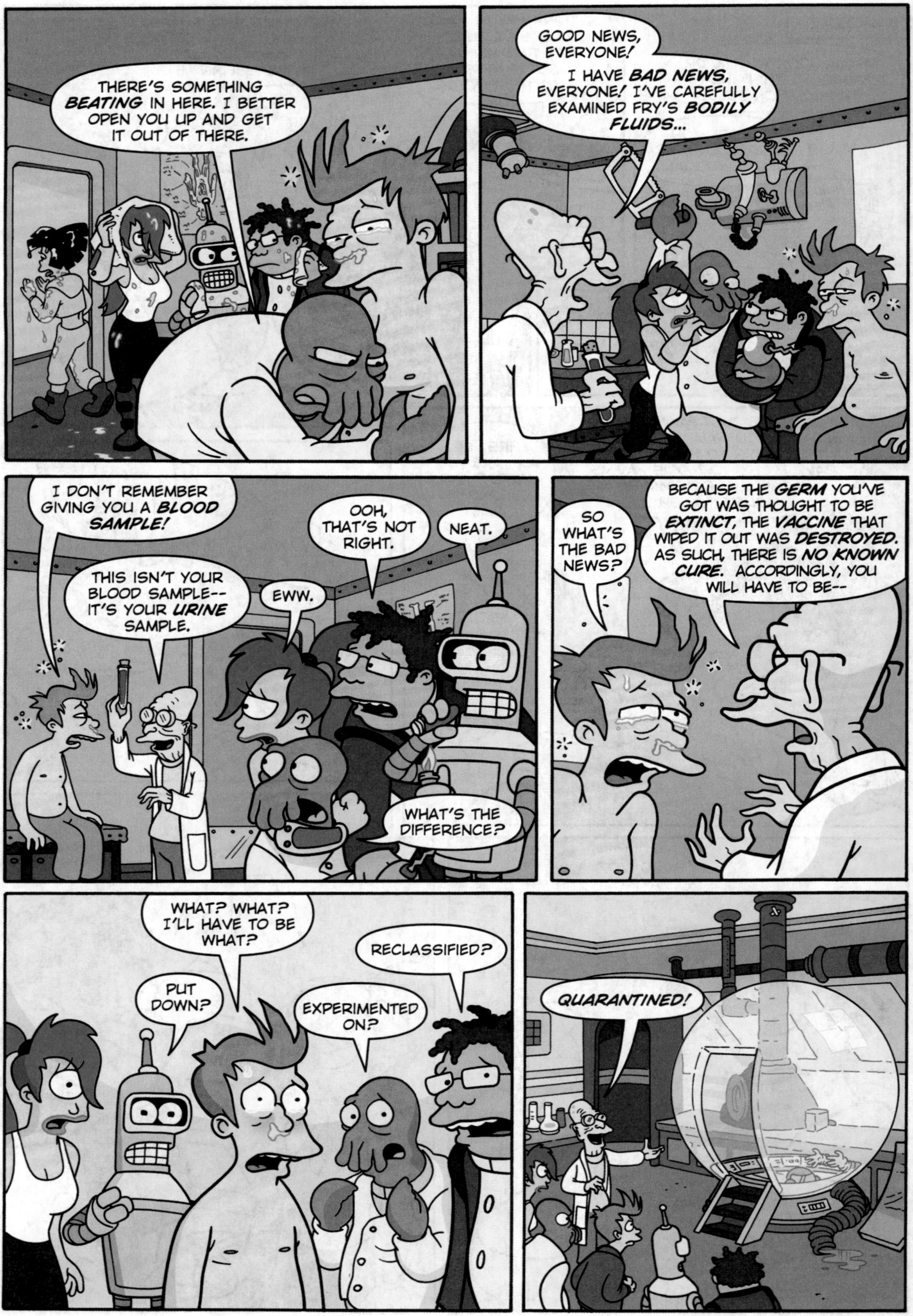
THERE'S SOMETHING *BEATING* IN HERE. I BETTER OPEN YOU UP AND GET IT OUT OF THERE.
GOOD NEWS, EVERYONE!
I HAVE *BAD NEWS*, EVERYONE! I'VE CAREFULLY EXAMINED FRY'S *BODILY FLUIDS*...
I DON'T REMEMBER GIVING YOU A *BLOOD SAMPLE!*
THIS ISN'T YOUR BLOOD SAMPLE-- IT'S YOUR *URINE* SAMPLE.
OOH, THAT'S NOT RIGHT.
NEAT.
EWW.
WHAT'S THE DIFFERENCE?
SO WHAT'S THE BAD NEWS?
BECAUSE THE *GERM* YOU'VE GOT WAS THOUGHT TO BE *EXTINCT*, THE *VACCINE* THAT WIPED IT OUT WAS *DESTROYED*. AS SUCH, THERE IS *NO KNOWN CURE*. ACCORDINGLY, YOU WILL HAVE TO BE--
WHAT? WHAT? I'LL HAVE TO BE WHAT?
PUT DOWN?
EXPERIMENTED ON?
RECLASSIFIED?
QUARANTINED!

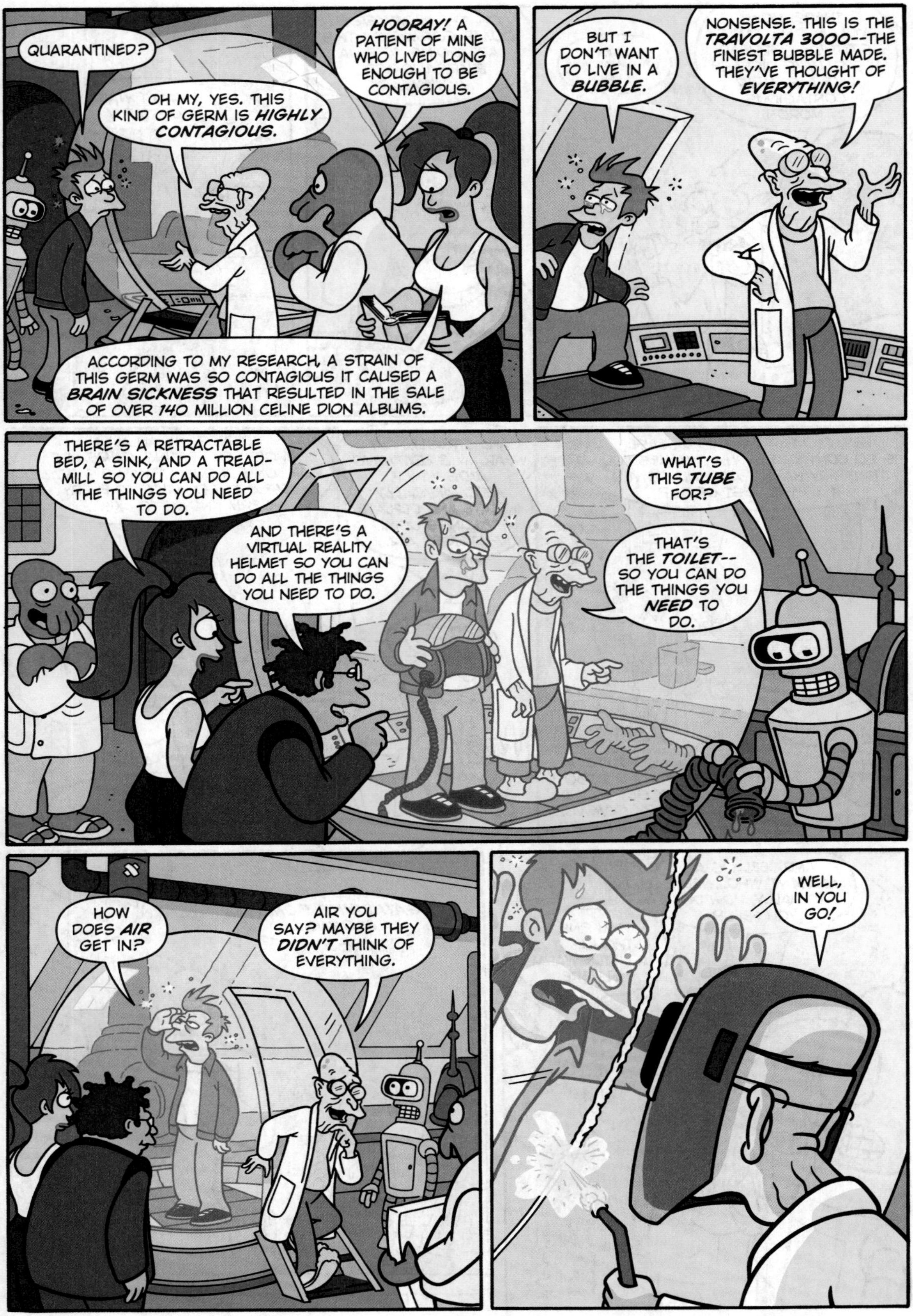
QUARANTINED?
OH MY, YES. THIS KIND OF GERM IS HIGHLY CONTAGIOUS.
HOORAY! A PATIENT OF MINE WHO LIVED LONG ENOUGH TO BE CONTAGIOUS.
ACCORDING TO MY RESEARCH, A STRAIN OF THIS GERM WAS SO CONTAGIOUS IT CAUSED A BRAIN SICKNESS THAT RESULTED IN THE SALE OF OVER 140 MILLION CELINE DION ALBUMS.
BUT I DON'T WANT TO LIVE IN A BUBBLE.
NONSENSE. THIS IS THE TRAVOLTA 3000--THE FINEST BUBBLE MADE. THEY'VE THOUGHT OF EVERYTHING!
THERE'S A RETRACTABLE BED, A SINK, AND A TREAD-MILL SO YOU CAN DO ALL THE THINGS YOU NEED TO DO.
AND THERE'S A VIRTUAL REALITY HELMET SO YOU CAN DO ALL THE THINGS YOU NEED TO DO.
WHAT'S THIS TUBE FOR?
THAT'S THE TOILET--SO YOU CAN DO THE THINGS YOU NEED TO DO.
HOW DOES AIR GET IN?
AIR YOU SAY? MAYBE THEY DIDN'T THINK OF EVERYTHING.
WELL, IN YOU GO!

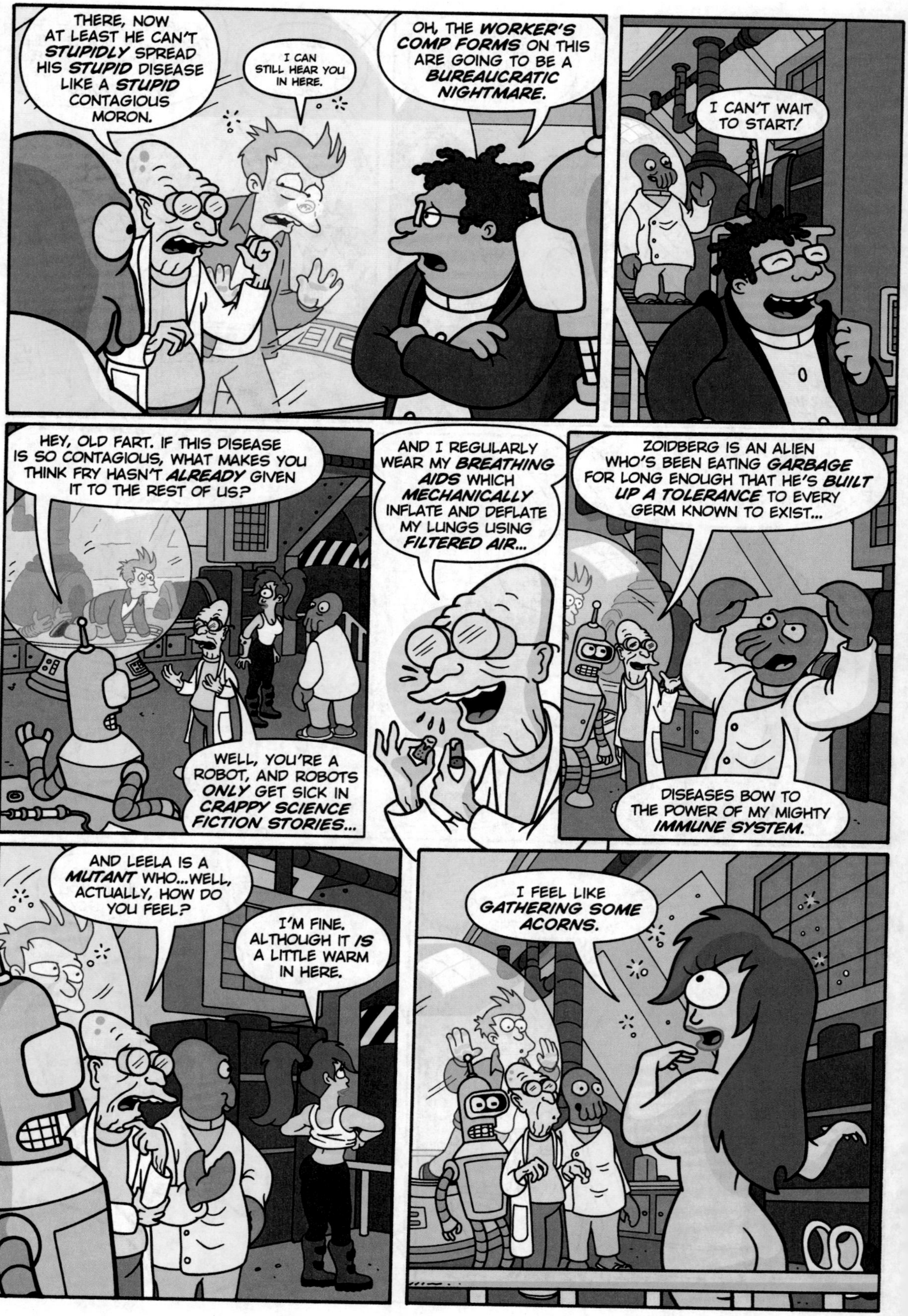
THERE, NOW AT LEAST HE CAN'T STUPIDLY SPREAD HIS STUPID DISEASE LIKE A STUPID CONTAGIOUS MORON.
I CAN STILL HEAR YOU IN HERE.
OH, THE WORKER'S COMP FORMS ON THIS ARE GOING TO BE A BUREAUCRATIC NIGHTMARE.
I CAN'T WAIT TO START!
HEY, OLD FART. IF THIS DISEASE IS SO CONTAGIOUS, WHAT MAKES YOU THINK FRY HASN'T ALREADY GIVEN IT TO THE REST OF US?
WELL, YOU'RE A ROBOT, AND ROBOTS ONLY GET SICK IN CRAPPY SCIENCE FICTION STORIES...
AND I REGULARLY WEAR MY BREATHING AIDS WHICH MECHANICALLY INFLATE AND DEFLATE MY LUNGS USING FILTERED AIR...
ZOIDBERG IS AN ALIEN WHO'S BEEN EATING GARBAGE FOR LONG ENOUGH THAT HE'S BUILT UP A TOLERANCE TO EVERY GERM KNOWN TO EXIST...
DISEASES BOW TO THE POWER OF MY MIGHTY IMMUNE SYSTEM.
AND LEELA IS A MUTANT WHO...WELL, ACTUALLY, HOW DO YOU FEEL?
I'M FINE. ALTHOUGH IT IS A LITTLE WARM IN HERE.
I FEEL LIKE GATHERING SOME ACORNS.

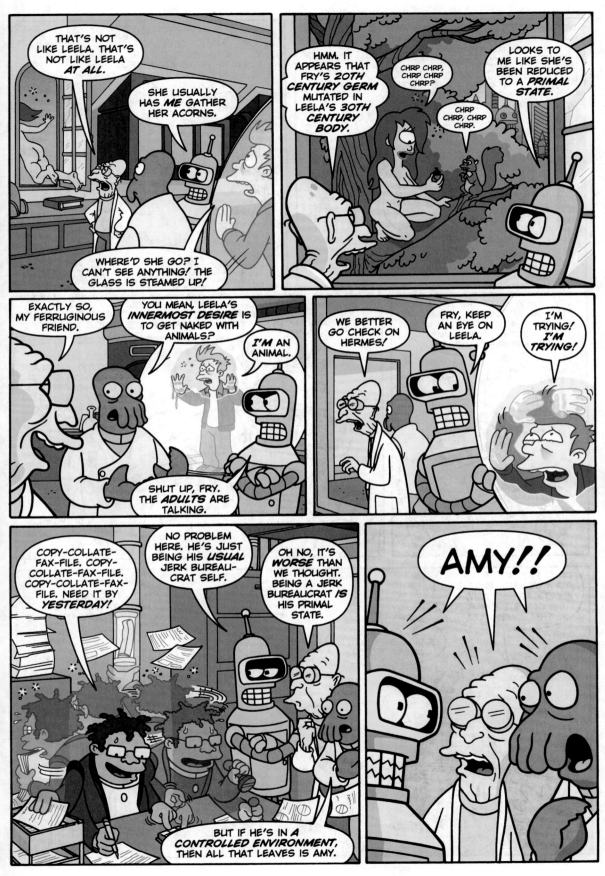

52

SOON AFTER...

WE'RE *TOO LATE*.

I *REALLY* WISH I FELT BETTER.

CAN WE HELP YOU?

WE'RE LOOKING FOR AMY WONG. OBVIOUSLY SHE'S BEEN HERE.

NO, SHE NEVER MADE IT. SOMEONE SAW HER AT *THE LIBRARY*. SHE SAID SHE WASN'T FEELING WELL.

SHE NEVER MADE IT? BUT THIS PARTY. IT'S SO...

THEN IT'S OFF TO THE LIBRARY. I REALLY MUST REMEMBER TO *RENEW* MY *SORORITY MEMBERSHIP*.

YOU CAN JUST LEAVE ME HERE TO DIE, ZOIDBERG.

DISAPPOINTING? YEAH. *USUALLY* OUR PARTIES ARE *REALLY WILD*.

THAT'S 'CAUSE AMY'S NOT HERE. IF YOU SEE HER, TELL HER WE MISS HER.

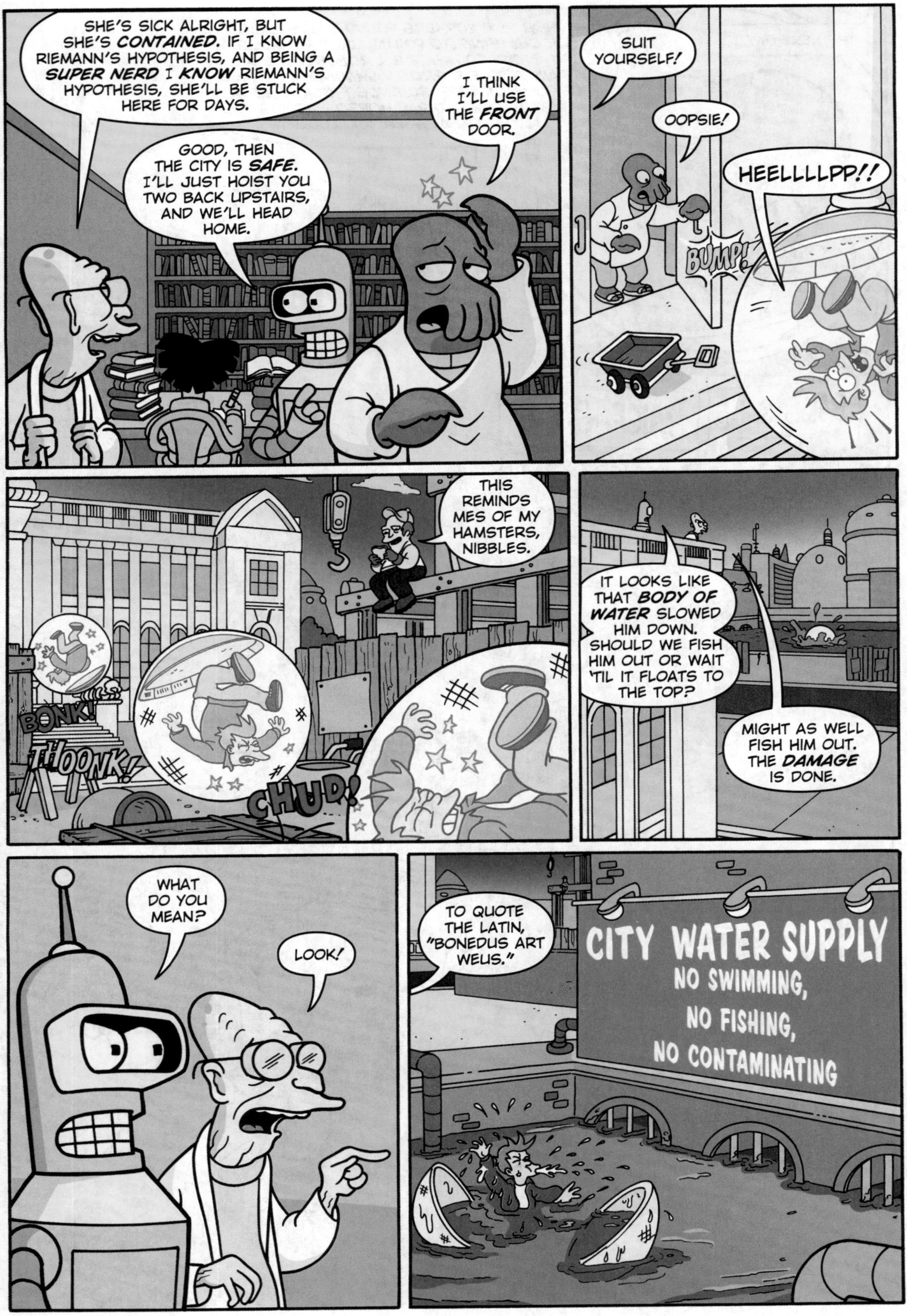

SHE'S SICK ALRIGHT, BUT SHE'S **CONTAINED.** IF I KNOW RIEMANN'S HYPOTHESIS, AND BEING A **SUPER NERD** I **KNOW** RIEMANN'S HYPOTHESIS, SHE'LL BE STUCK HERE FOR DAYS.
GOOD, THEN THE CITY IS **SAFE.** I'LL JUST HOIST YOU TWO BACK UPSTAIRS, AND WE'LL HEAD HOME.
I THINK I'LL USE THE **FRONT** DOOR.
SUIT YOURSELF!
OOPSIE!
HEELLLLPP!!
BUMP!
THIS REMINDS MES OF MY HAMSTERS, NIBBLES.
BONK!
THOONK!
CHUD!
IT LOOKS LIKE THAT **BODY OF WATER** SLOWED HIM DOWN. SHOULD WE FISH HIM OUT OR WAIT 'TIL IT FLOATS TO THE TOP?
MIGHT AS WELL FISH HIM OUT. THE **DAMAGE** IS DONE.
WHAT DO YOU MEAN?
LOOK!
TO QUOTE THE LATIN, "BONEDUS ART WEUS."
CITY WATER SUPPLY
NO SWIMMING,
NO FISHING,
NO CONTAMINATING

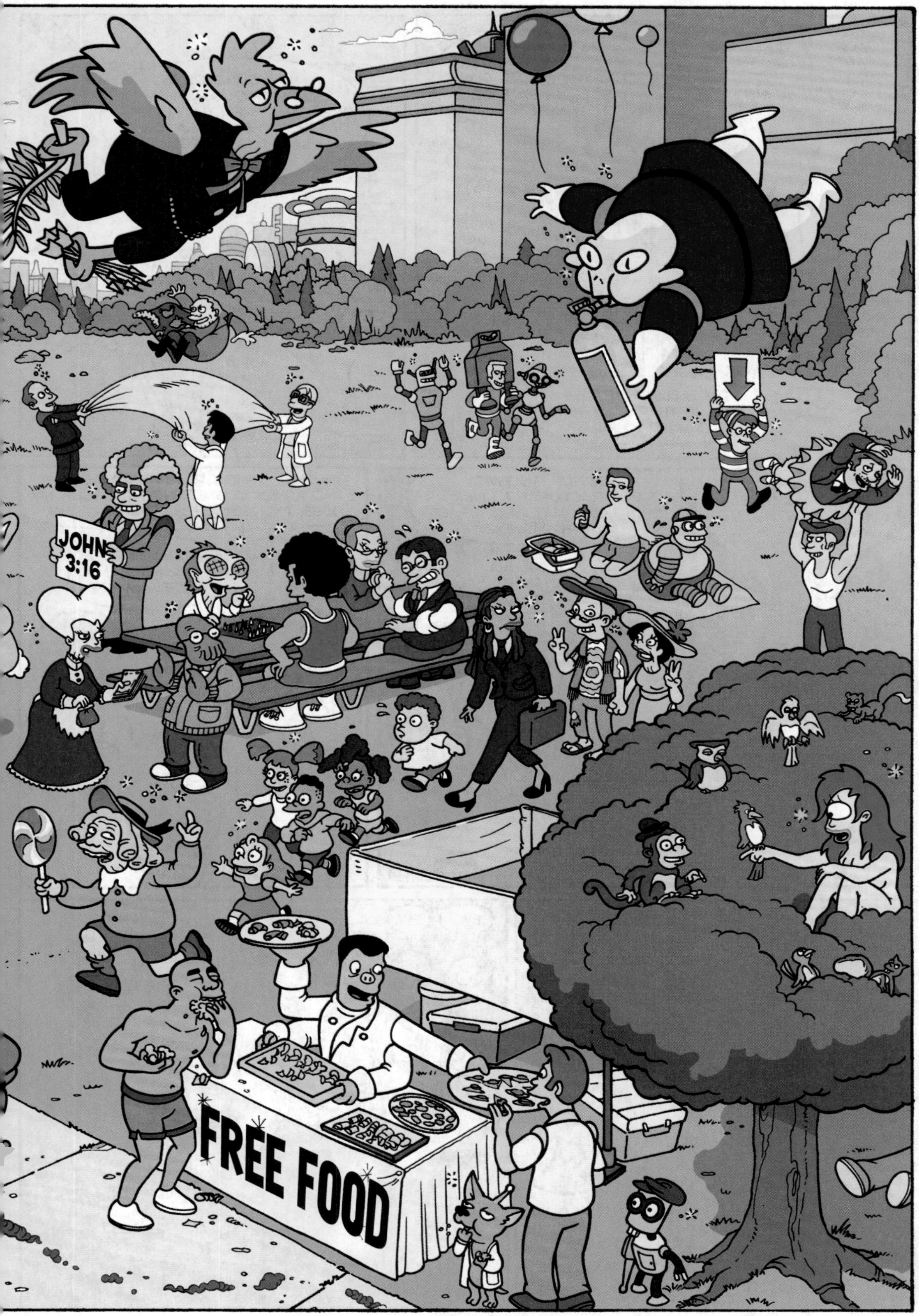
JOHN
3:16
FREE FOOD

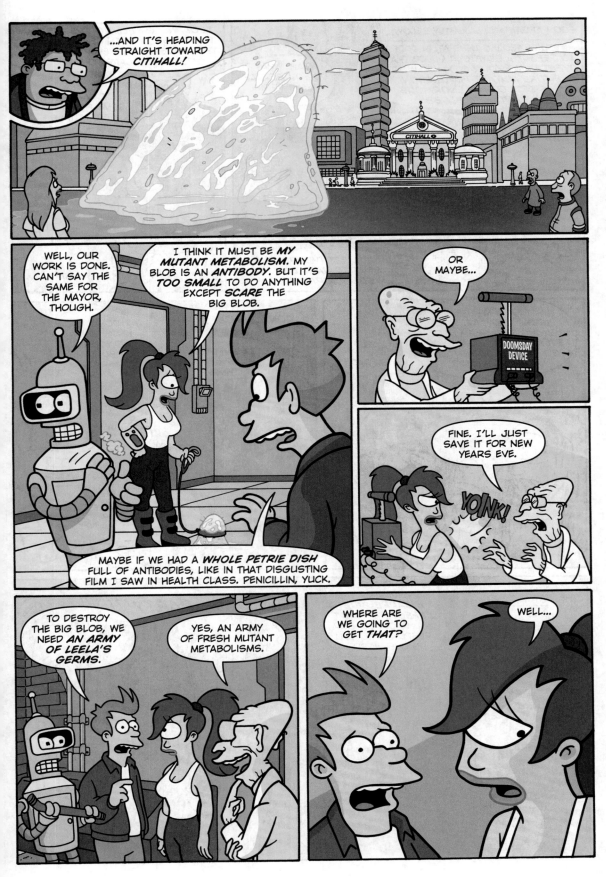

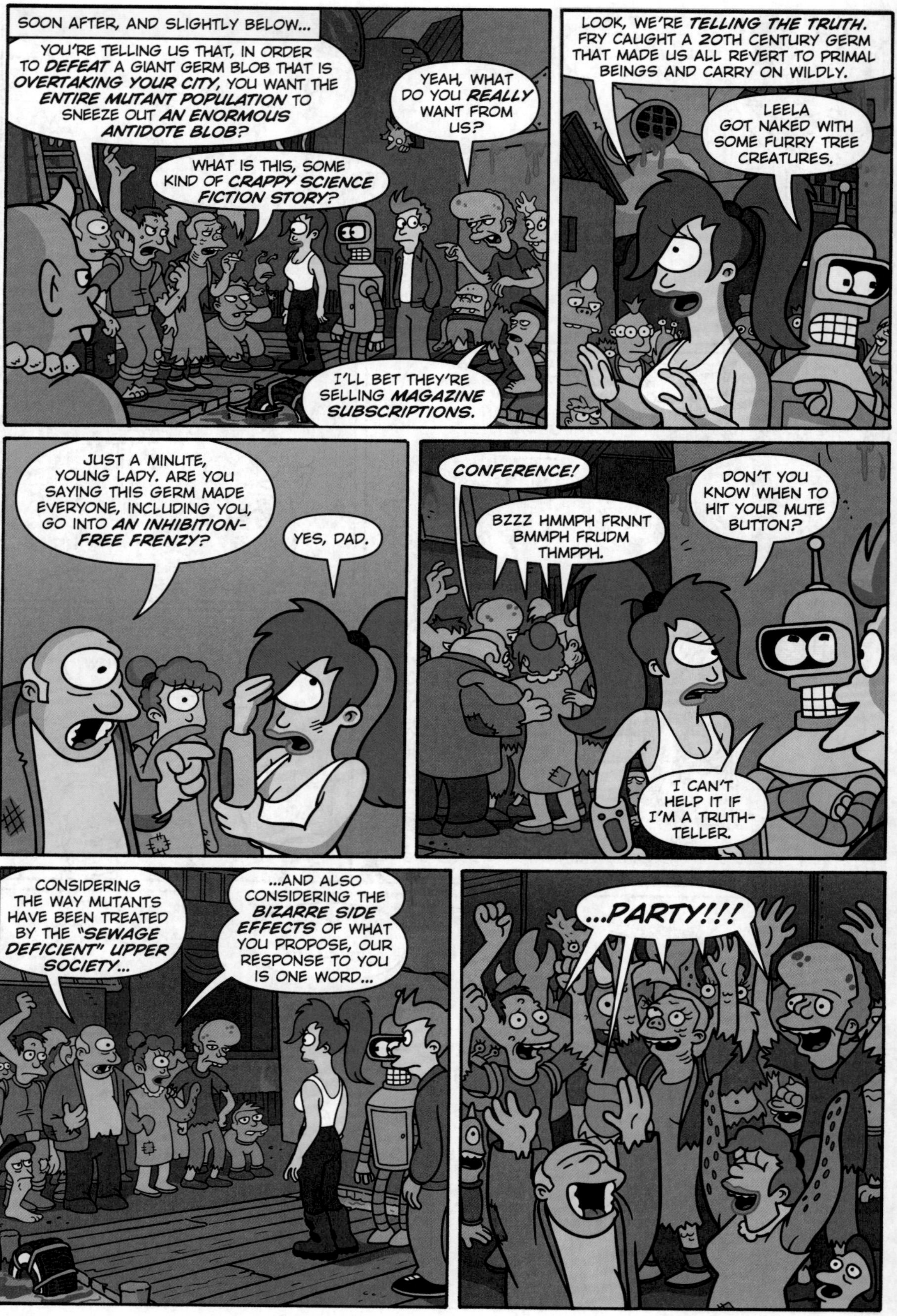
SOON AFTER, AND SLIGHTLY BELOW...
YOU'RE TELLING US THAT, IN ORDER TO DEFEAT A GIANT GERM BLOB THAT IS OVERTAKING YOUR CITY, YOU WANT THE ENTIRE MUTANT POPULATION TO SNEEZE OUT AN ENORMOUS ANTIDOTE BLOB?
YEAH, WHAT DO YOU REALLY WANT FROM US?
WHAT IS THIS, SOME KIND OF CRAPPY SCIENCE FICTION STORY?
I'LL BET THEY'RE SELLING MAGAZINE SUBSCRIPTIONS.
LOOK, WE'RE TELLING THE TRUTH. FRY CAUGHT A 20TH CENTURY GERM THAT MADE US ALL REVERT TO PRIMAL BEINGS AND CARRY ON WILDLY.
LEELA GOT NAKED WITH SOME FURRY TREE CREATURES.
JUST A MINUTE, YOUNG LADY. ARE YOU SAYING THIS GERM MADE EVERYONE, INCLUDING YOU, GO INTO AN INHIBITION-FREE FRENZY?
YES, DAD.
CONFERENCE!
BZZZ HMMPH FRNNT BMMPH FRUDM THMPPH.
DON'T YOU KNOW WHEN TO HIT YOUR MUTE BUTTON?
I CAN'T HELP IT IF I'M A TRUTH-TELLER.
CONSIDERING THE WAY MUTANTS HAVE BEEN TREATED BY THE "SEWAGE DEFICIENT" UPPER SOCIETY...
...AND ALSO CONSIDERING THE BIZARRE SIDE EFFECTS OF WHAT YOU PROPOSE, OUR RESPONSE TO YOU IS ONE WORD...
...PARTY!!!

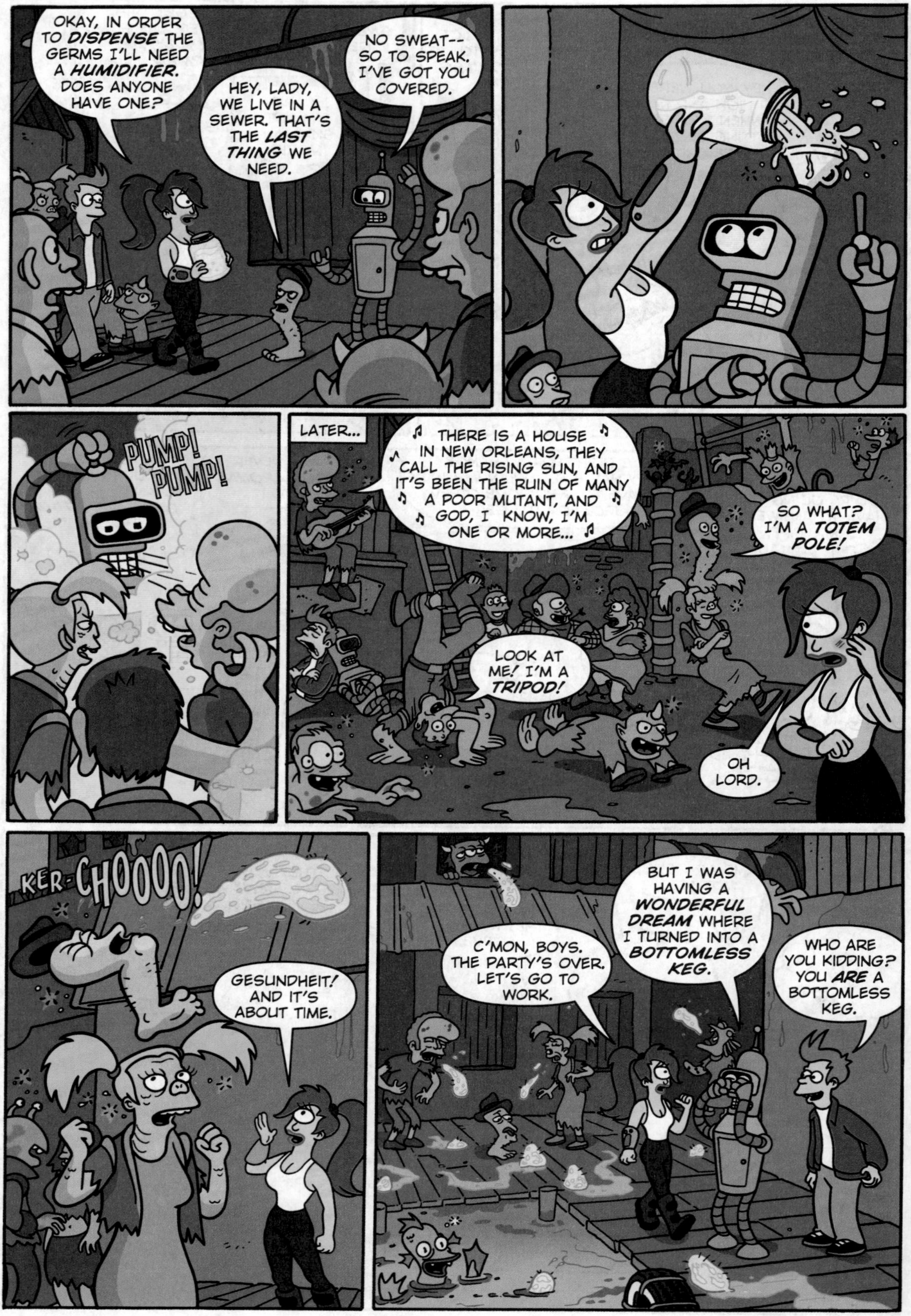
OKAY, IN ORDER TO DISPENSE THE GERMS I'LL NEED A HUMIDIFIER. DOES ANYONE HAVE ONE?
HEY, LADY, WE LIVE IN A SEWER. THAT'S THE LAST THING WE NEED.
NO SWEAT-- SO TO SPEAK. I'VE GOT YOU COVERED.
PUMP! PUMP!
LATER...
♫ THERE IS A HOUSE IN NEW ORLEANS, THEY CALL THE RISING SUN, AND IT'S BEEN THE RUIN OF MANY A POOR MUTANT, AND GOD, I KNOW, I'M ONE OR MORE... ♫
SO WHAT? I'M A TOTEM POLE!
LOOK AT ME! I'M A TRIPOD!
OH LORD.
KER-CHOOOO!
GESUNDHEIT! AND IT'S ABOUT TIME.
C'MON, BOYS. THE PARTY'S OVER. LET'S GO TO WORK.
BUT I WAS HAVING A WONDERFUL DREAM WHERE I TURNED INTO A BOTTOMLESS KEG.
WHO ARE YOU KIDDING? YOU ARE A BOTTOMLESS KEG.

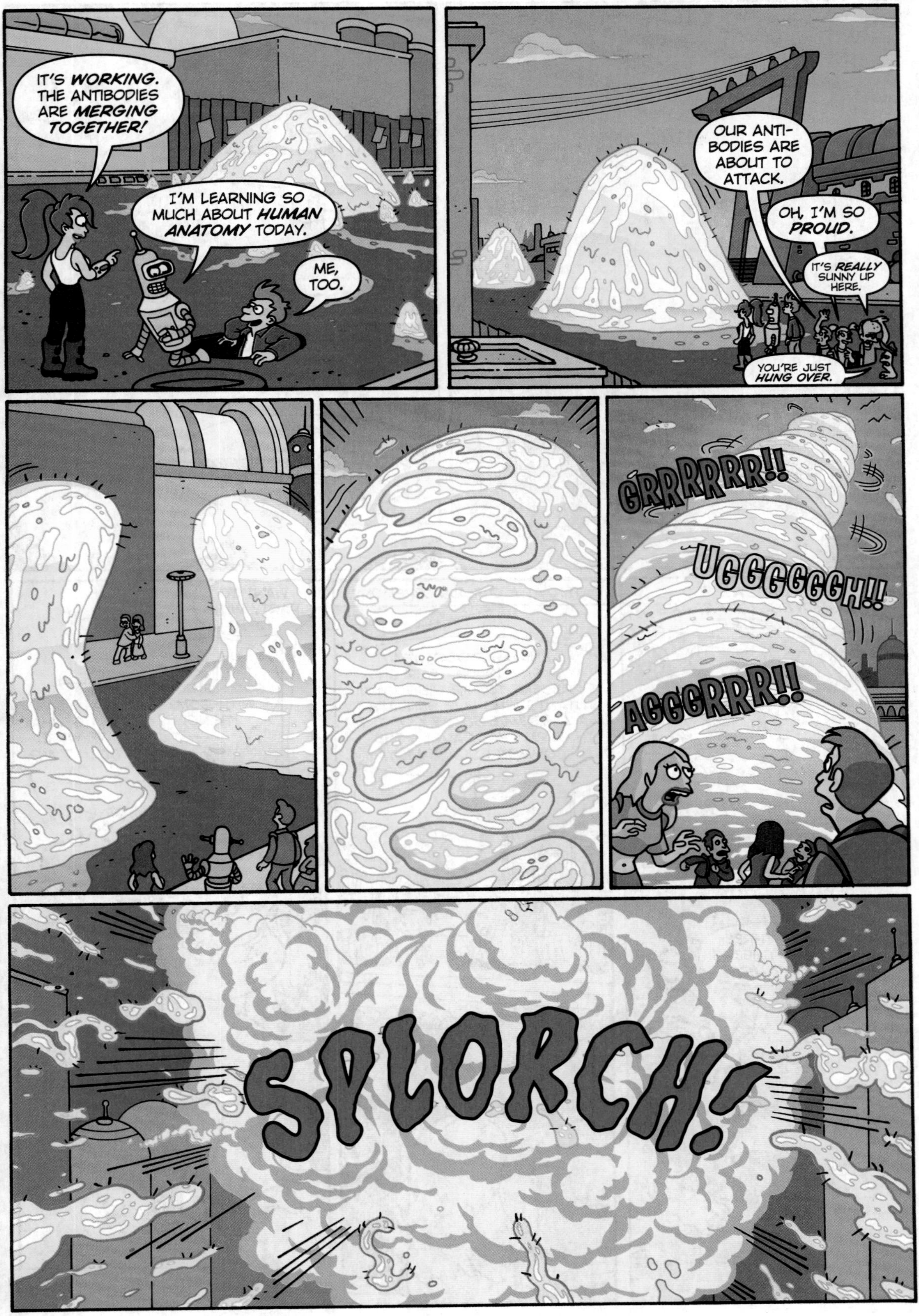
IT'S *WORKING*. THE ANTIBODIES ARE *MERGING TOGETHER!*
I'M LEARNING SO MUCH ABOUT *HUMAN ANATOMY* TODAY.
ME, TOO.
OUR ANTI-BODIES ARE ABOUT TO ATTACK.
OH, I'M SO *PROUD*.
IT'S *REALLY* SUNNY UP HERE.
YOU'RE JUST *HUNG OVER*.
GRRRRRR!!
UGGGGGGH!!
AGGGRRR!!
SPLORCH!

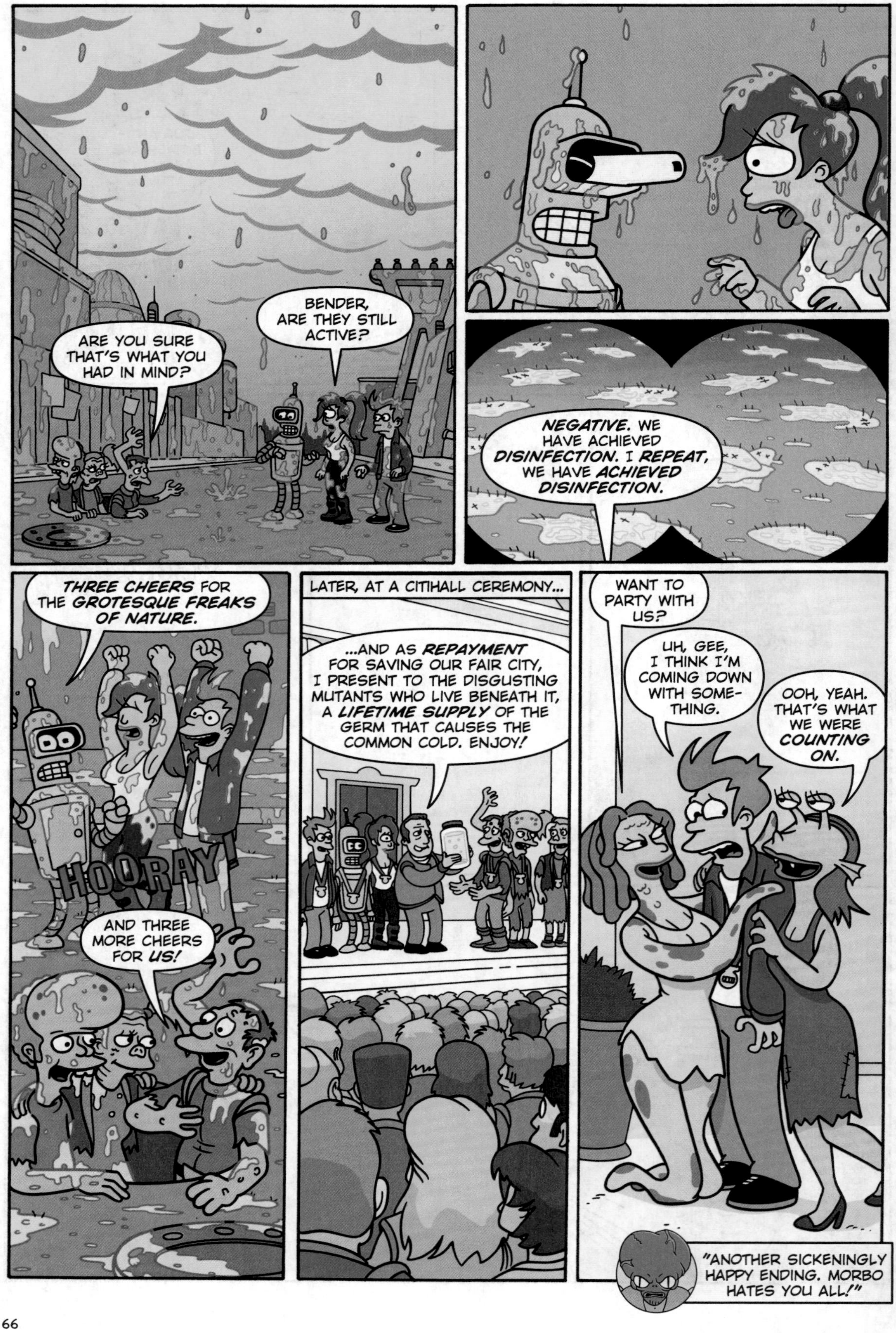
ARE YOU SURE THAT'S WHAT YOU HAD IN MIND?
BENDER, ARE THEY STILL ACTIVE?
NEGATIVE. WE HAVE ACHIEVED DISINFECTION. I REPEAT, WE HAVE ACHIEVED DISINFECTION.
THREE CHEERS FOR THE GROTESQUE FREAKS OF NATURE.
HOORAY!
AND THREE MORE CHEERS FOR US!
LATER, AT A CITIHALL CEREMONY...
...AND AS REPAYMENT FOR SAVING OUR FAIR CITY, I PRESENT TO THE DISGUSTING MUTANTS WHO LIVE BENEATH IT, A LIFETIME SUPPLY OF THE GERM THAT CAUSES THE COMMON COLD. ENJOY!
WANT TO PARTY WITH US?
UH, GEE, I THINK I'M COMING DOWN WITH SOME- THING.
OOH, YEAH. THAT'S WHAT WE WERE COUNTING ON.
"ANOTHER SICKENINGLY HAPPY ENDING. MORBO HATES YOU ALL!"

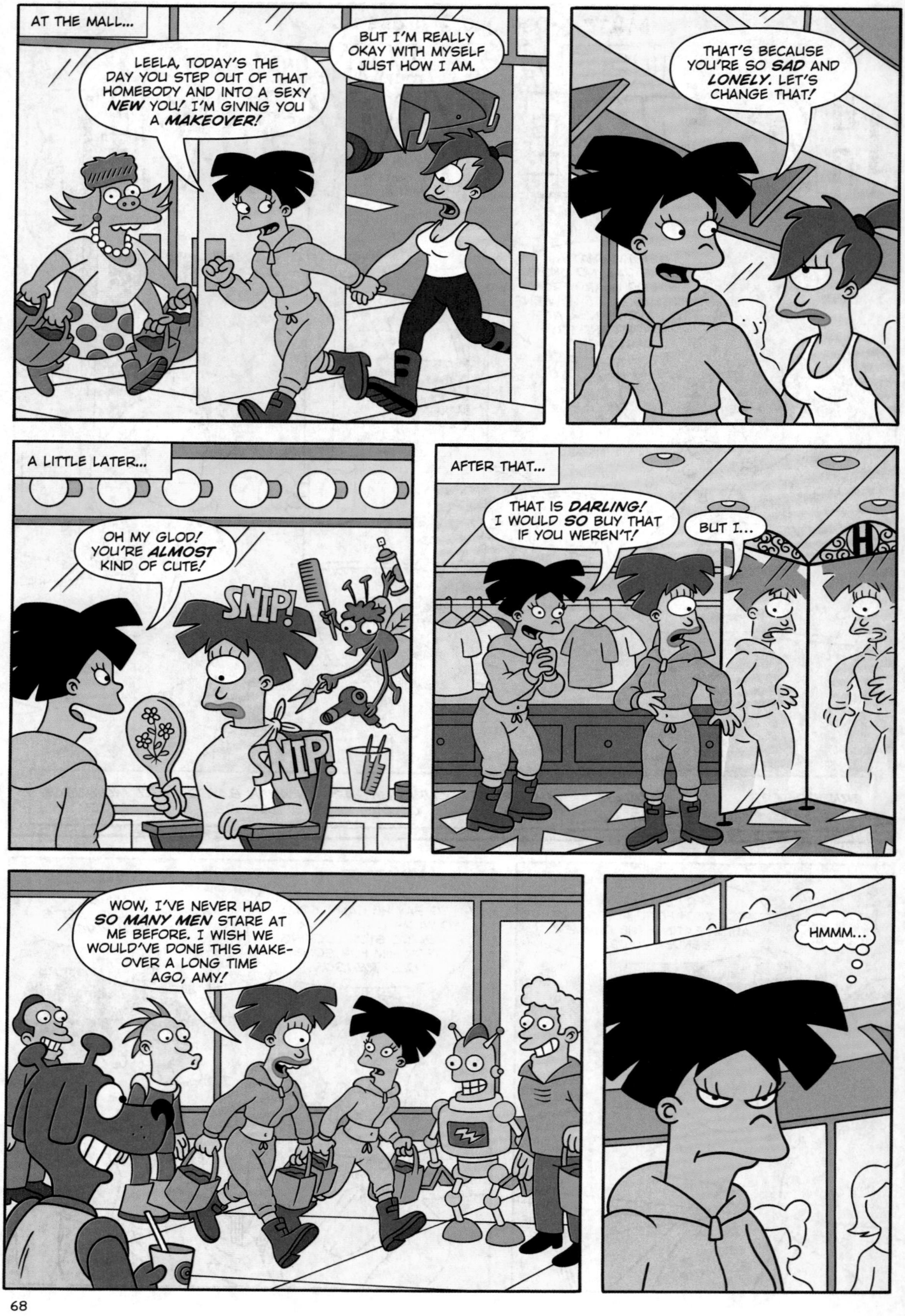
AT THE MALL...
LEELA, TODAY'S THE DAY YOU STEP OUT OF THAT HOMEBODY AND INTO A SEXY NEW YOU! I'M GIVING YOU A MAKEOVER!
BUT I'M REALLY OKAY WITH MYSELF JUST HOW I AM.
THAT'S BECAUSE YOU'RE SO SAD AND LONELY. LET'S CHANGE THAT!
A LITTLE LATER...
OH MY GLOD! YOU'RE ALMOST KIND OF CUTE!
SNIP!
SNIP!
AFTER THAT...
THAT IS DARLING! I WOULD SO BUY THAT IF YOU WEREN'T!
BUT I...
WOW, I'VE NEVER HAD SO MANY MEN STARE AT ME BEFORE. I WISH WE WOULD'VE DONE THIS MAKE-OVER A LONG TIME AGO, AMY!
HMMM...

69

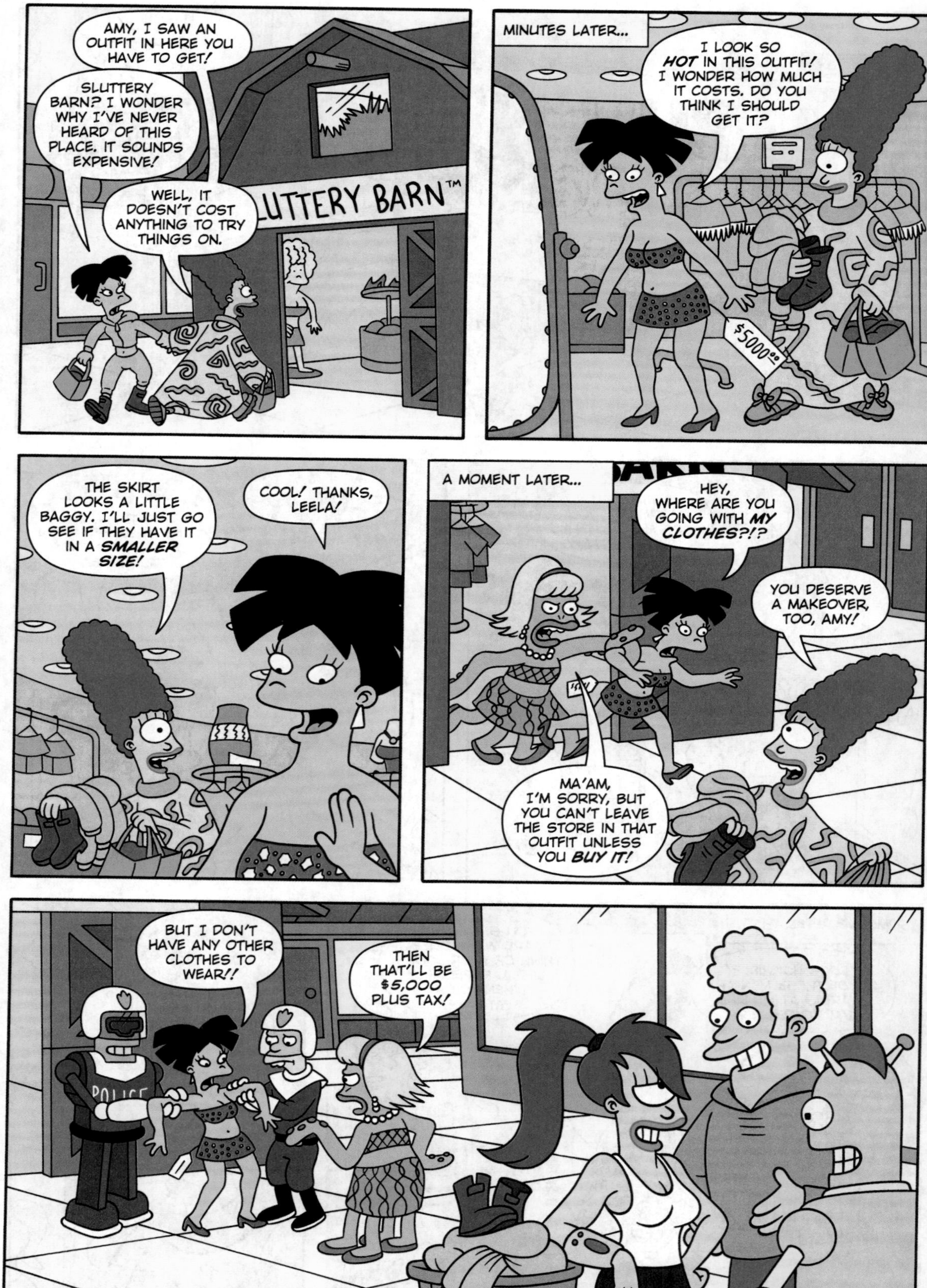
AMY, I SAW AN OUTFIT IN HERE YOU HAVE TO GET!
SLUTTERY BARN? I WONDER WHY I'VE NEVER HEARD OF THIS PLACE. IT SOUNDS EXPENSIVE!
WELL, IT DOESN'T COST ANYTHING TO TRY THINGS ON.
LUTTERY BARN™
MINUTES LATER...
I LOOK SO **HOT** IN THIS OUTFIT! I WONDER HOW MUCH IT COSTS. DO YOU THINK I SHOULD GET IT?
$5000.00
THE SKIRT LOOKS A LITTLE BAGGY. I'LL JUST GO SEE IF THEY HAVE IT IN A ***SMALLER SIZE!***
COOL! THANKS, LEELA!
A MOMENT LATER...
HEY, WHERE ARE YOU GOING WITH ***MY CLOTHES?!?***
YOU DESERVE A MAKEOVER, TOO, AMY!
MA'AM, I'M SORRY, BUT YOU CAN'T LEAVE THE STORE IN THAT OUTFIT UNLESS YOU ***BUY IT!***
BUT I DON'T HAVE ANY OTHER CLOTHES TO WEAR!!
THEN THAT'LL BE $5,000 PLUS TAX!
POLICE
TRASH
THE END

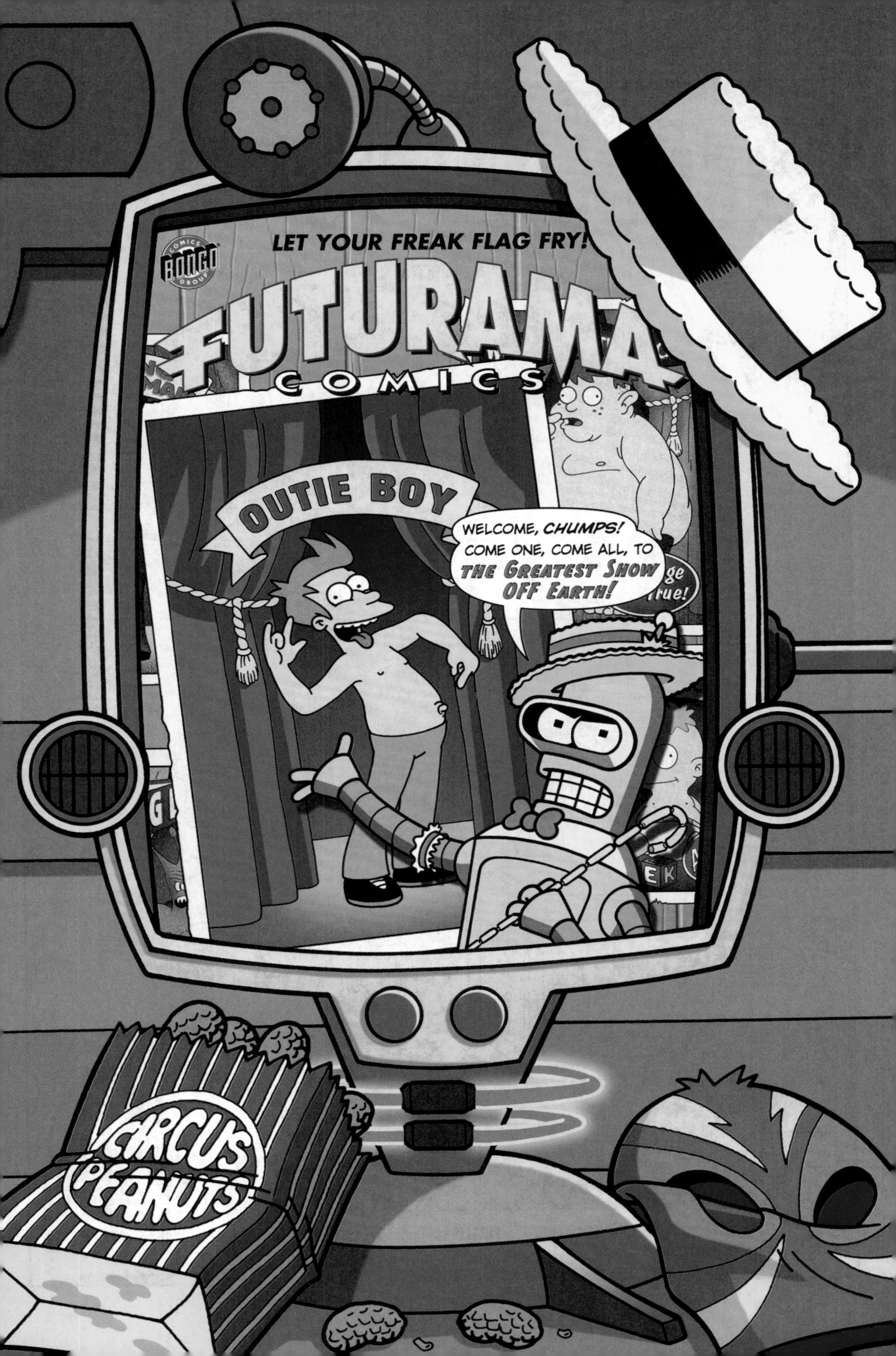
LET YOUR FREAK FLAG FRY!
BONGO COMICS GROUP
FUTURAMA COMICS
OUTIE BOY
WELCOME, CHUMPS! COME ONE, COME ALL, TO THE GREATEST SHOW OFF EARTH!
CIRCUS PEANUTS

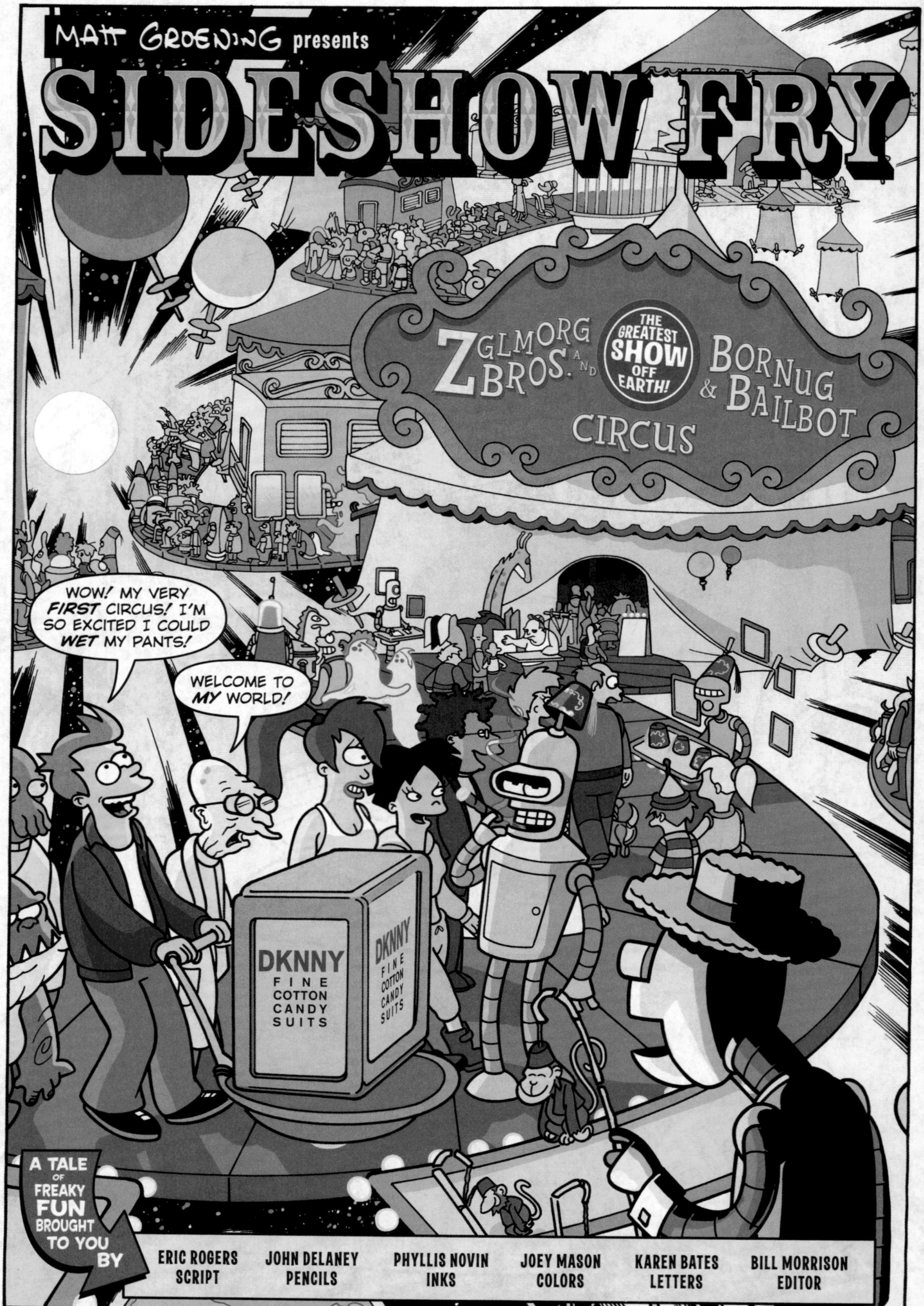
MATT GROENING presents
SIDESHOW FRY
ZGLMORG BROS. AND BORNUG & BAILBOT CIRCUS
THE GREATEST SHOW OFF EARTH!
WOW! MY VERY FIRST CIRCUS! I'M SO EXCITED I COULD WET MY PANTS!
WELCOME TO MY WORLD!
DKNNY FINE COTTON CANDY SUITS
A TALE OF FREAKY FUN BROUGHT TO YOU BY
ERIC ROGERS SCRIPT
JOHN DELANEY PENCILS
PHYLLIS NOVIN INKS
JOEY MASON COLORS
KAREN BATES LETTERS
BILL MORRISON EDITOR

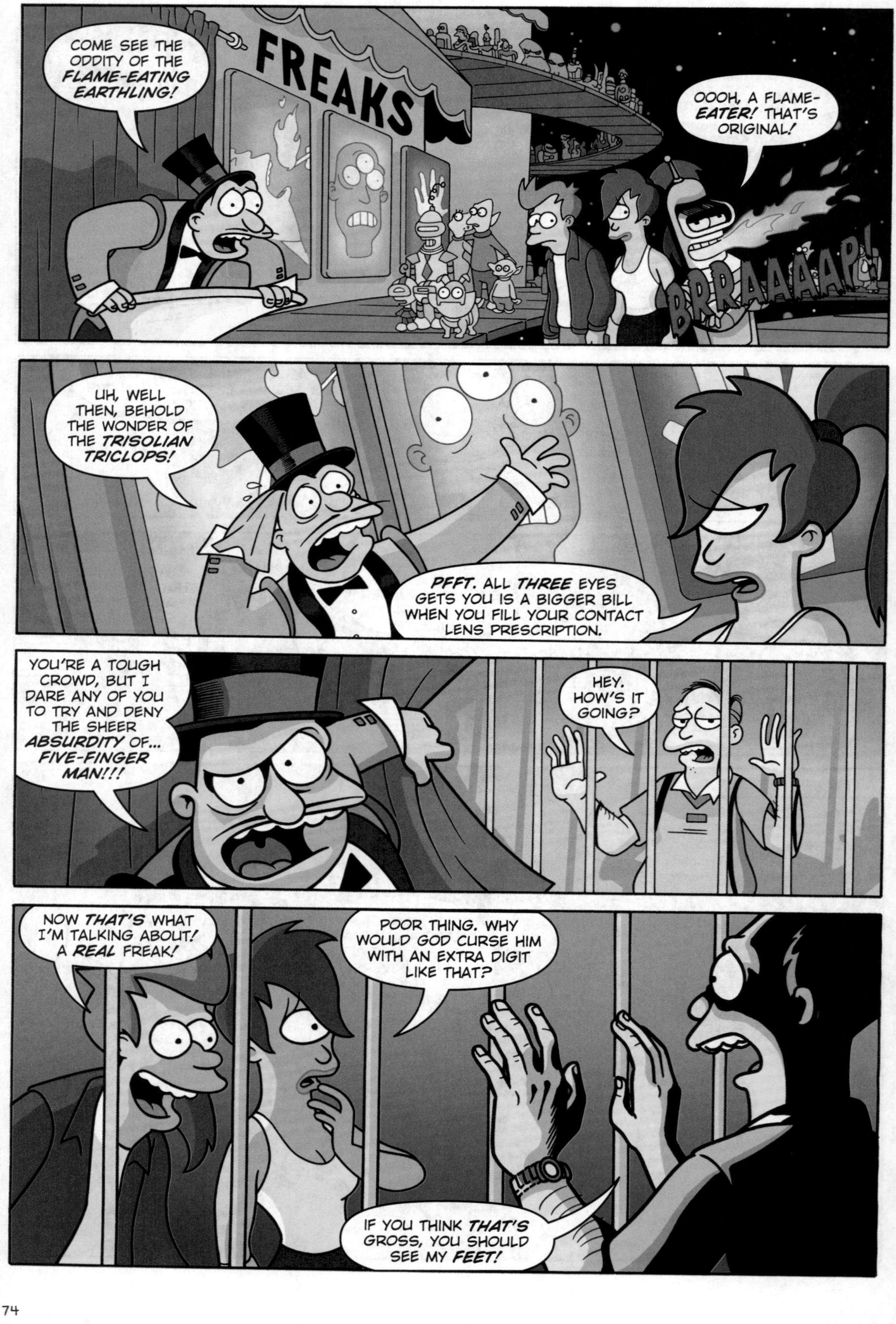

COME SEE THE ODDITY OF THE FLAME-EATING EARTHLING!
FREAKS
OOOH, A FLAME-EATER! THAT'S ORIGINAL!
BRRAAAAP!
UH, WELL THEN, BEHOLD THE WONDER OF THE TRISOLIAN TRICLOPS!
PFFT. ALL THREE EYES GETS YOU IS A BIGGER BILL WHEN YOU FILL YOUR CONTACT LENS PRESCRIPTION.
YOU'RE A TOUGH CROWD, BUT I DARE ANY OF YOU TO TRY AND DENY THE SHEER ABSURDITY OF... FIVE-FINGER MAN!!!
HEY. HOW'S IT GOING?
NOW THAT'S WHAT I'M TALKING ABOUT! A REAL FREAK!
POOR THING. WHY WOULD GOD CURSE HIM WITH AN EXTRA DIGIT LIKE THAT?
IF YOU THINK THAT'S GROSS, YOU SHOULD SEE MY FEET!

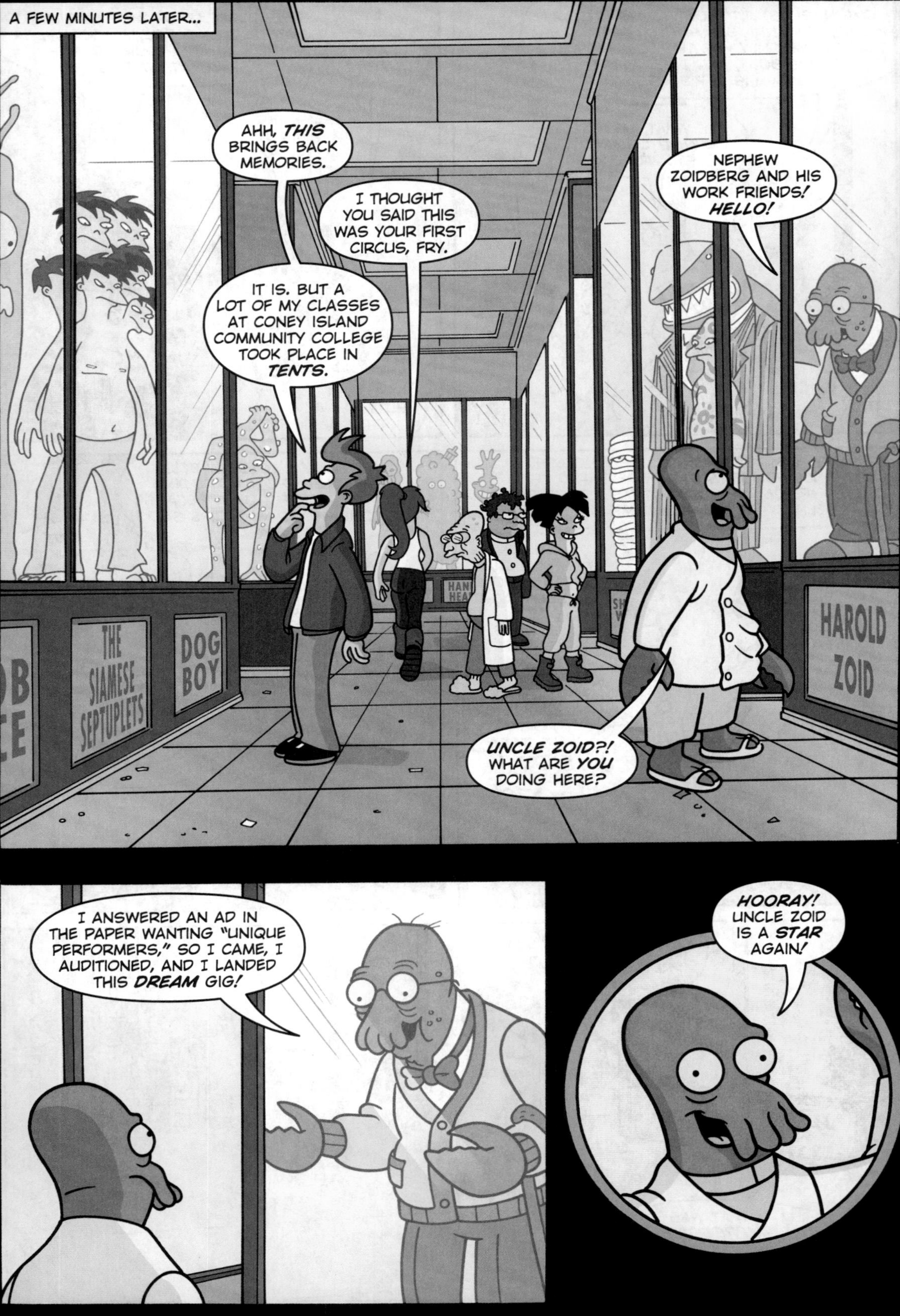
A FEW MINUTES LATER...
AHH, THIS BRINGS BACK MEMORIES.
I THOUGHT YOU SAID THIS WAS YOUR FIRST CIRCUS, FRY.
IT IS. BUT A LOT OF MY CLASSES AT CONEY ISLAND COMMUNITY COLLEGE TOOK PLACE IN TENTS.
NEPHEW ZOIDBERG AND HIS WORK FRIENDS! HELLO!
THE SIAMESE SEPTUPLETS
DOG BOY
HAROLD ZOID
UNCLE ZOID?! WHAT ARE YOU DOING HERE?
I ANSWERED AN AD IN THE PAPER WANTING "UNIQUE PERFORMERS," SO I CAME, I AUDITIONED, AND I LANDED THIS DREAM GIG!
HOORAY! UNCLE ZOID IS A STAR AGAIN!

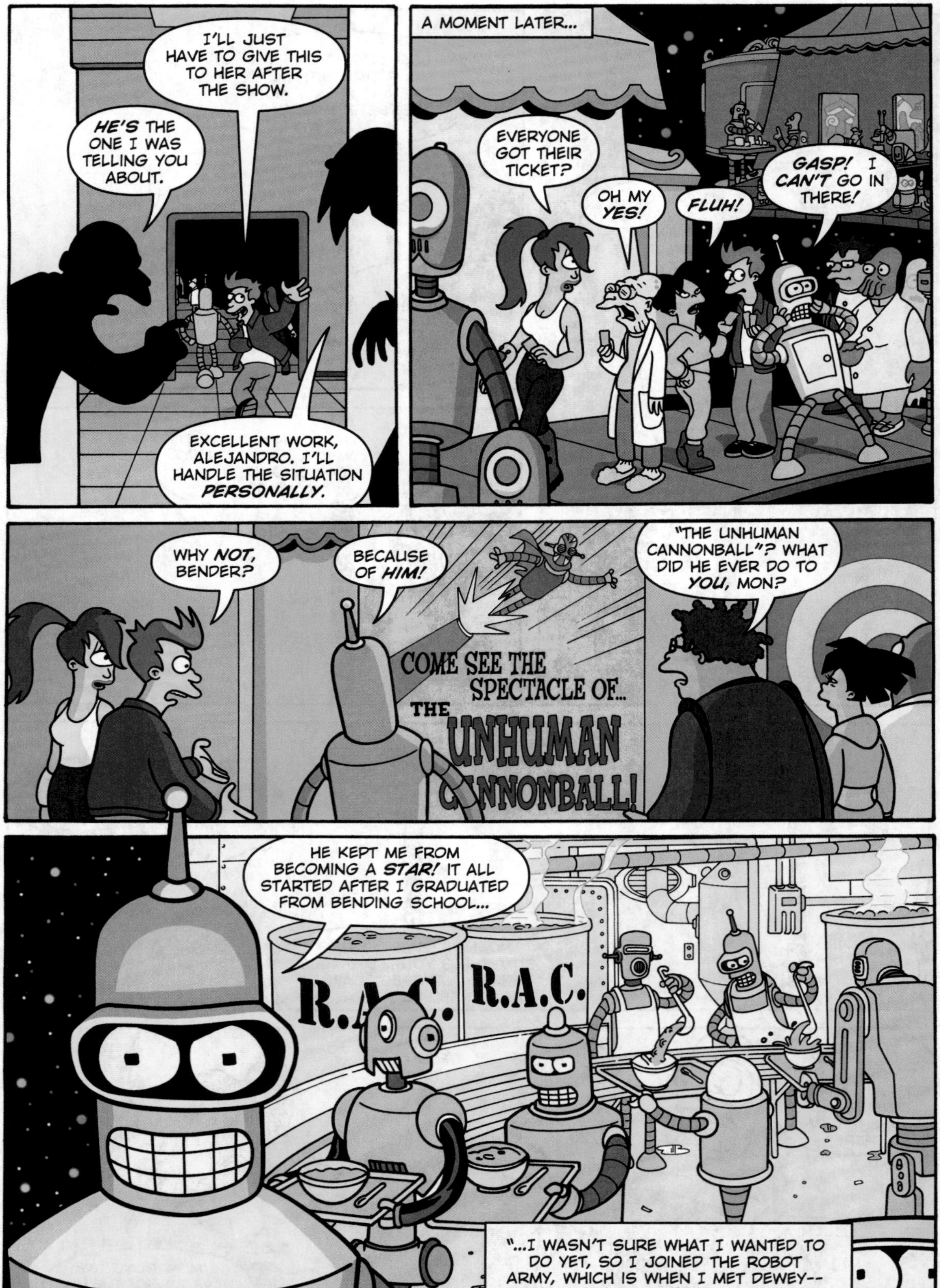
I'LL JUST HAVE TO GIVE THIS TO HER AFTER THE SHOW.
HE'S THE ONE I WAS TELLING YOU ABOUT.
EXCELLENT WORK, ALEJANDRO. I'LL HANDLE THE SITUATION PERSONALLY.
A MOMENT LATER...
EVERYONE GOT THEIR TICKET?
OH MY YES!
FLUH!
GASP! I CAN'T GO IN THERE!
WHY NOT, BENDER?
BECAUSE OF HIM!
COME SEE THE SPECTACLE OF... THE UNHUMAN CANNONBALL!
"THE UNHUMAN CANNONBALL"? WHAT DID HE EVER DO TO YOU, MON?
HE KEPT ME FROM BECOMING A STAR! IT ALL STARTED AFTER I GRADUATED FROM BENDING SCHOOL...
R.A.C.
R.A.C.
"...I WASN'T SURE WHAT I WANTED TO DO YET, SO I JOINED THE ROBOT ARMY, WHICH IS WHEN I MET DEWEY--NOW KNOWN AS "THE UNHUMAN CANNONBALL"--AT 'BOT CAMP."

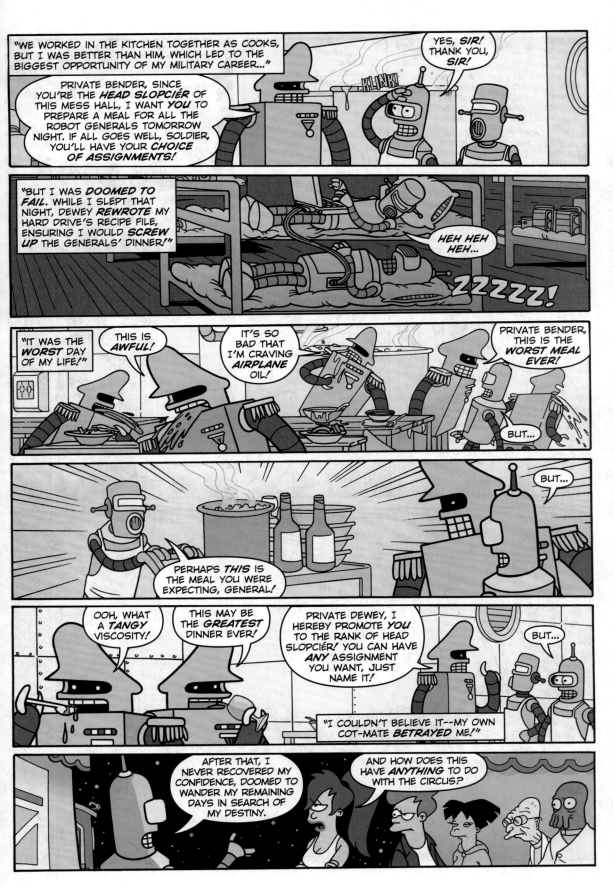

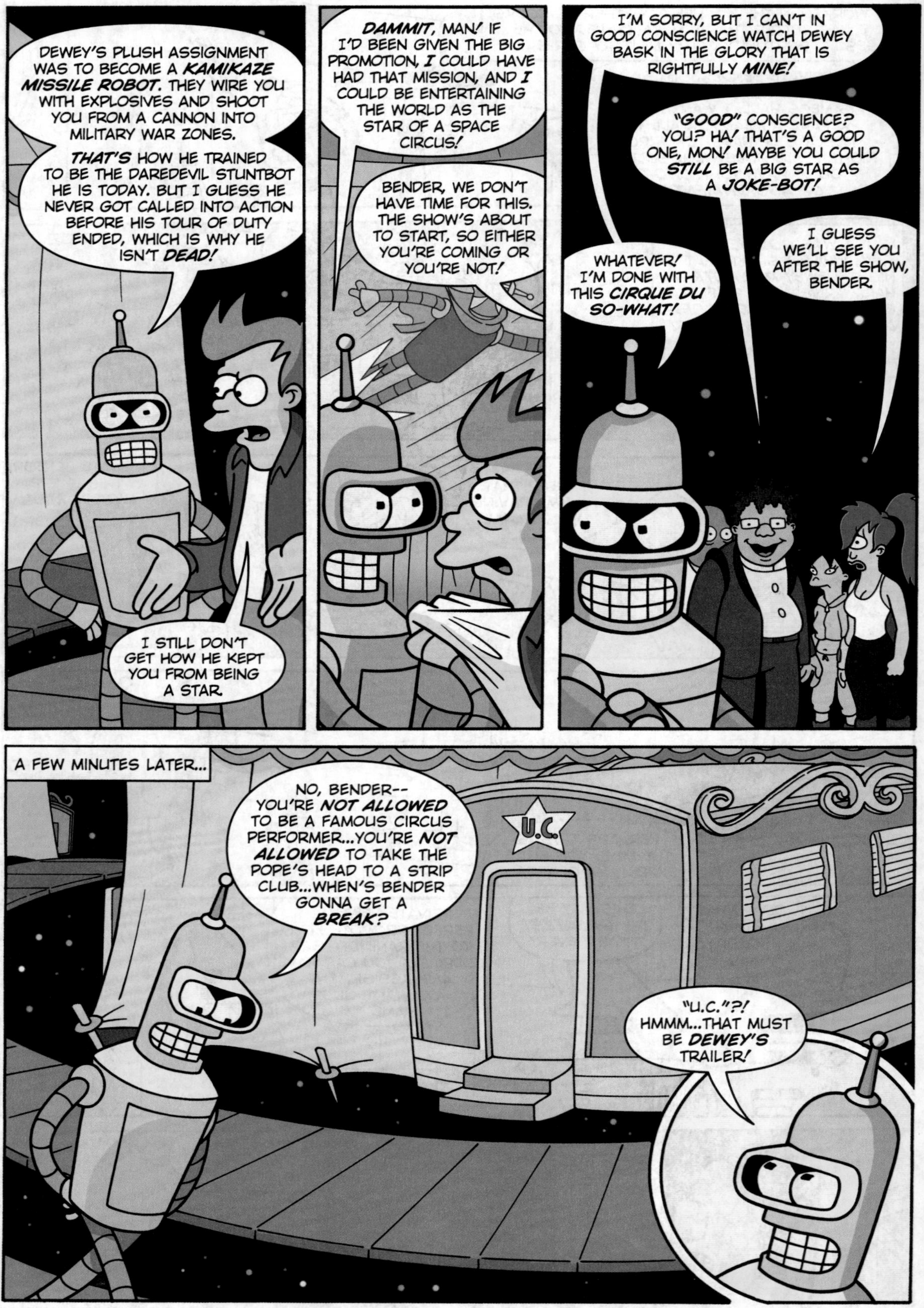
DEWEY'S PLUSH ASSIGNMENT WAS TO BECOME A KAMIKAZE MISSILE ROBOT. THEY WIRE YOU WITH EXPLOSIVES AND SHOOT YOU FROM A CANNON INTO MILITARY WAR ZONES.
THAT'S HOW HE TRAINED TO BE THE DAREDEVIL STUNTBOT HE IS TODAY. BUT I GUESS HE NEVER GOT CALLED INTO ACTION BEFORE HIS TOUR OF DUTY ENDED, WHICH IS WHY HE ISN'T DEAD!
I STILL DON'T GET HOW HE KEPT YOU FROM BEING A STAR.
DAMMIT, MAN! IF I'D BEEN GIVEN THE BIG PROMOTION, I COULD HAVE HAD THAT MISSION, AND I COULD BE ENTERTAINING THE WORLD AS THE STAR OF A SPACE CIRCUS!
BENDER, WE DON'T HAVE TIME FOR THIS. THE SHOW'S ABOUT TO START, SO EITHER YOU'RE COMING OR YOU'RE NOT!
I'M SORRY, BUT I CAN'T IN GOOD CONSCIENCE WATCH DEWEY BASK IN THE GLORY THAT IS RIGHTFULLY MINE!
"GOOD" CONSCIENCE? YOU? HA! THAT'S A GOOD ONE, MON! MAYBE YOU COULD STILL BE A BIG STAR AS A JOKE-BOT!
WHATEVER! I'M DONE WITH THIS CIRQUE DU SO-WHAT!
I GUESS WE'LL SEE YOU AFTER THE SHOW, BENDER.
A FEW MINUTES LATER...
NO, BENDER-- YOU'RE NOT ALLOWED TO BE A FAMOUS CIRCUS PERFORMER...YOU'RE NOT ALLOWED TO TAKE THE POPE'S HEAD TO A STRIP CLUB...WHEN'S BENDER GONNA GET A BREAK?
U.C.
"U.C."?! HMMM...THAT MUST BE DEWEY'S TRAILER!

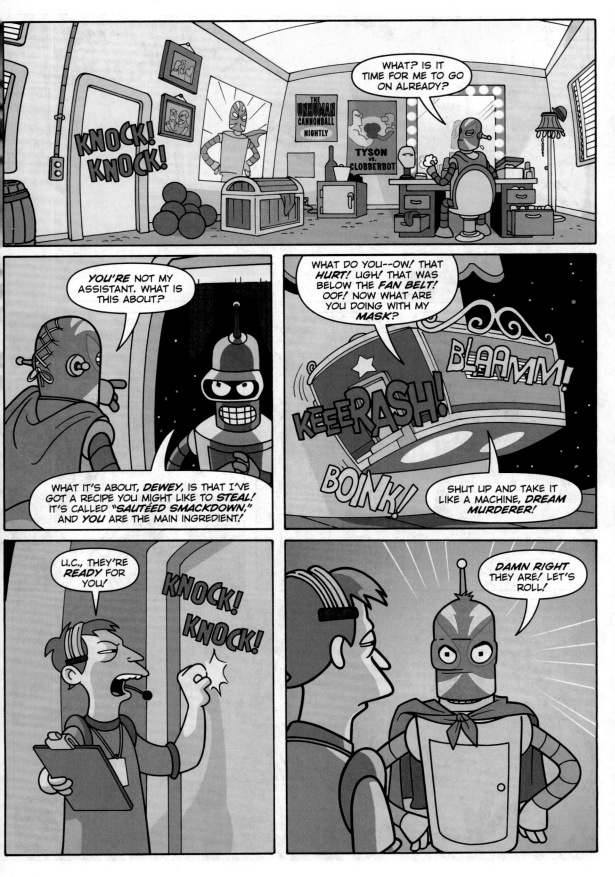

82

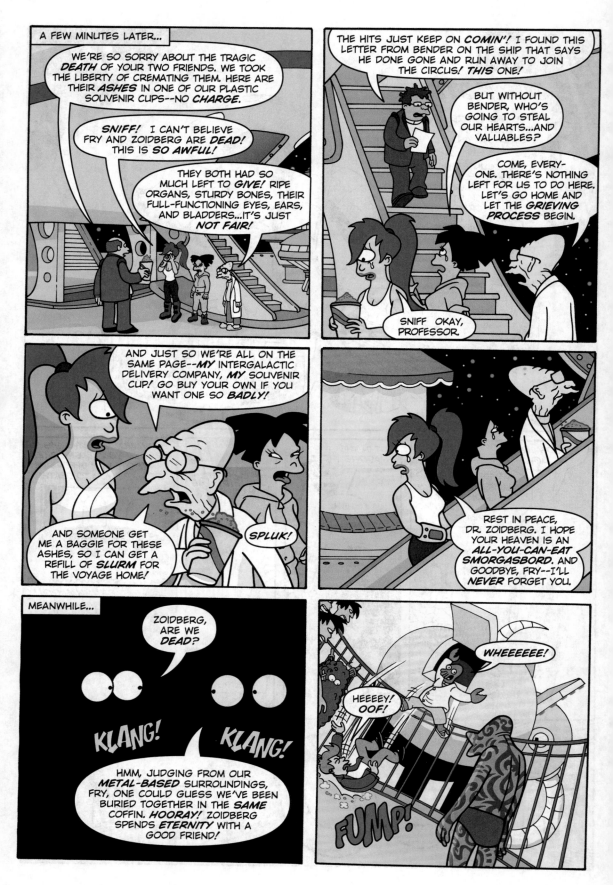

85

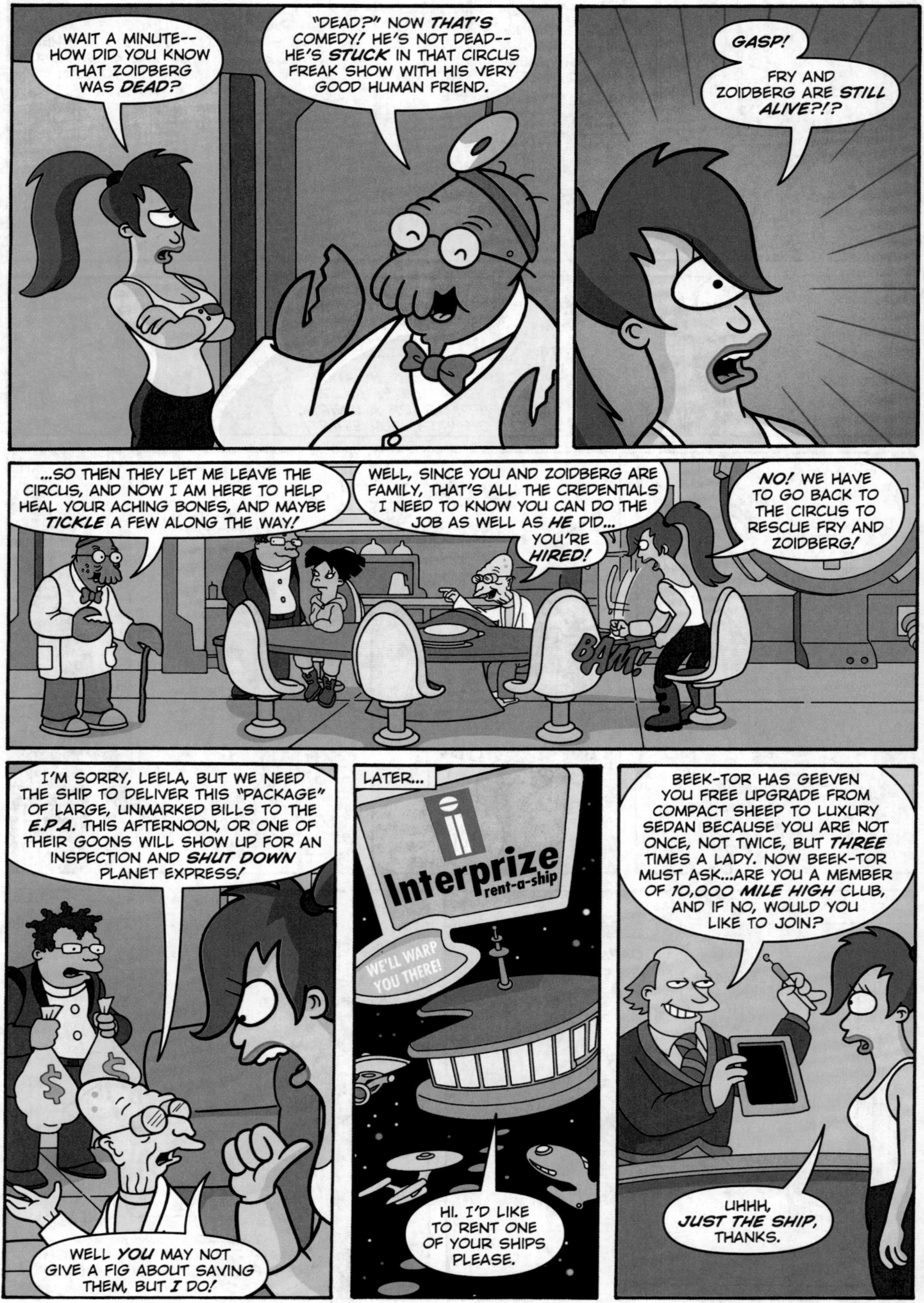

WAIT A MINUTE--HOW DID YOU KNOW THAT ZOIDBERG WAS *DEAD?*
"DEAD?" NOW *THAT'S* COMEDY! HE'S NOT DEAD--HE'S *STUCK* IN THAT CIRCUS FREAK SHOW WITH HIS VERY GOOD HUMAN FRIEND.
GASP!
FRY AND ZOIDBERG ARE *STILL ALIVE?!?*
...SO THEN THEY LET ME LEAVE THE CIRCUS, AND NOW I AM HERE TO HELP HEAL YOUR ACHING BONES, AND MAYBE *TICKLE* A FEW ALONG THE WAY!
WELL, SINCE YOU AND ZOIDBERG ARE FAMILY, THAT'S ALL THE CREDENTIALS I NEED TO KNOW YOU CAN DO THE JOB AS WELL AS *HE* DID...
YOU'RE *HIRED!*
NO! WE HAVE TO GO BACK TO THE CIRCUS TO RESCUE FRY AND ZOIDBERG!
BAM!
I'M SORRY, LEELA, BUT WE NEED THE SHIP TO DELIVER THIS "PACKAGE" OF LARGE, UNMARKED BILLS TO THE *E.P.A.* THIS AFTERNOON, OR ONE OF THEIR GOONS WILL SHOW UP FOR AN INSPECTION AND *SHUT DOWN* PLANET EXPRESS!
WELL *YOU* MAY NOT GIVE A FIG ABOUT SAVING THEM, BUT *I* DO!
LATER...
Interprize rent-a-ship
WE'LL WARP YOU THERE!
HI. I'D LIKE TO RENT ONE OF YOUR SHIPS PLEASE.
BEEK-TOR HAS GEEVEN YOU FREE UPGRADE FROM COMPACT SHEEP TO LUXURY SEDAN BECAUSE YOU ARE NOT ONCE, NOT TWICE, BUT *THREE* TIMES A LADY. NOW BEEK-TOR MUST ASK...ARE YOU A MEMBER OF *10,000 MILE HIGH* CLUB, AND IF NO, WOULD YOU LIKE TO JOIN?
UHHH, *JUST THE SHIP,* THANKS.

87

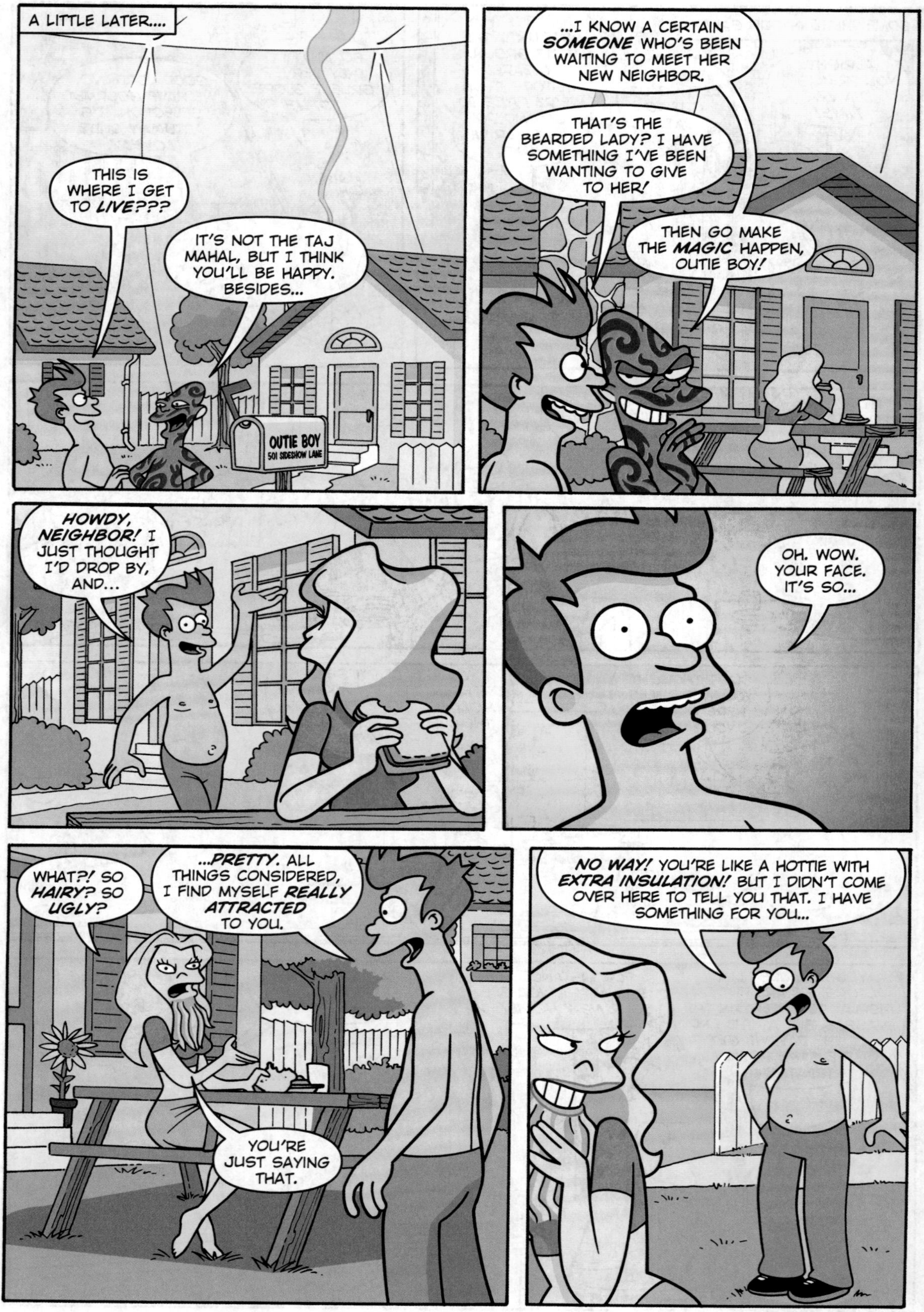
A LITTLE LATER....
THIS IS WHERE I GET TO LIVE???
IT'S NOT THE TAJ MAHAL, BUT I THINK YOU'LL BE HAPPY. BESIDES...
OUTIE BOY
501 SIDESHOW LANE
...I KNOW A CERTAIN SOMEONE WHO'S BEEN WAITING TO MEET HER NEW NEIGHBOR.
THAT'S THE BEARDED LADY? I HAVE SOMETHING I'VE BEEN WANTING TO GIVE TO HER!
THEN GO MAKE THE MAGIC HAPPEN, OUTIE BOY!
HOWDY, NEIGHBOR! I JUST THOUGHT I'D DROP BY, AND...
OH. WOW. YOUR FACE. IT'S SO...
WHAT?! SO HAIRY? SO UGLY?
...PRETTY. ALL THINGS CONSIDERED, I FIND MYSELF REALLY ATTRACTED TO YOU.
YOU'RE JUST SAYING THAT.
NO WAY! YOU'RE LIKE A HOTTIE WITH EXTRA INSULATION! BUT I DIDN'T COME OVER HERE TO TELL YOU THAT. I HAVE SOMETHING FOR YOU...

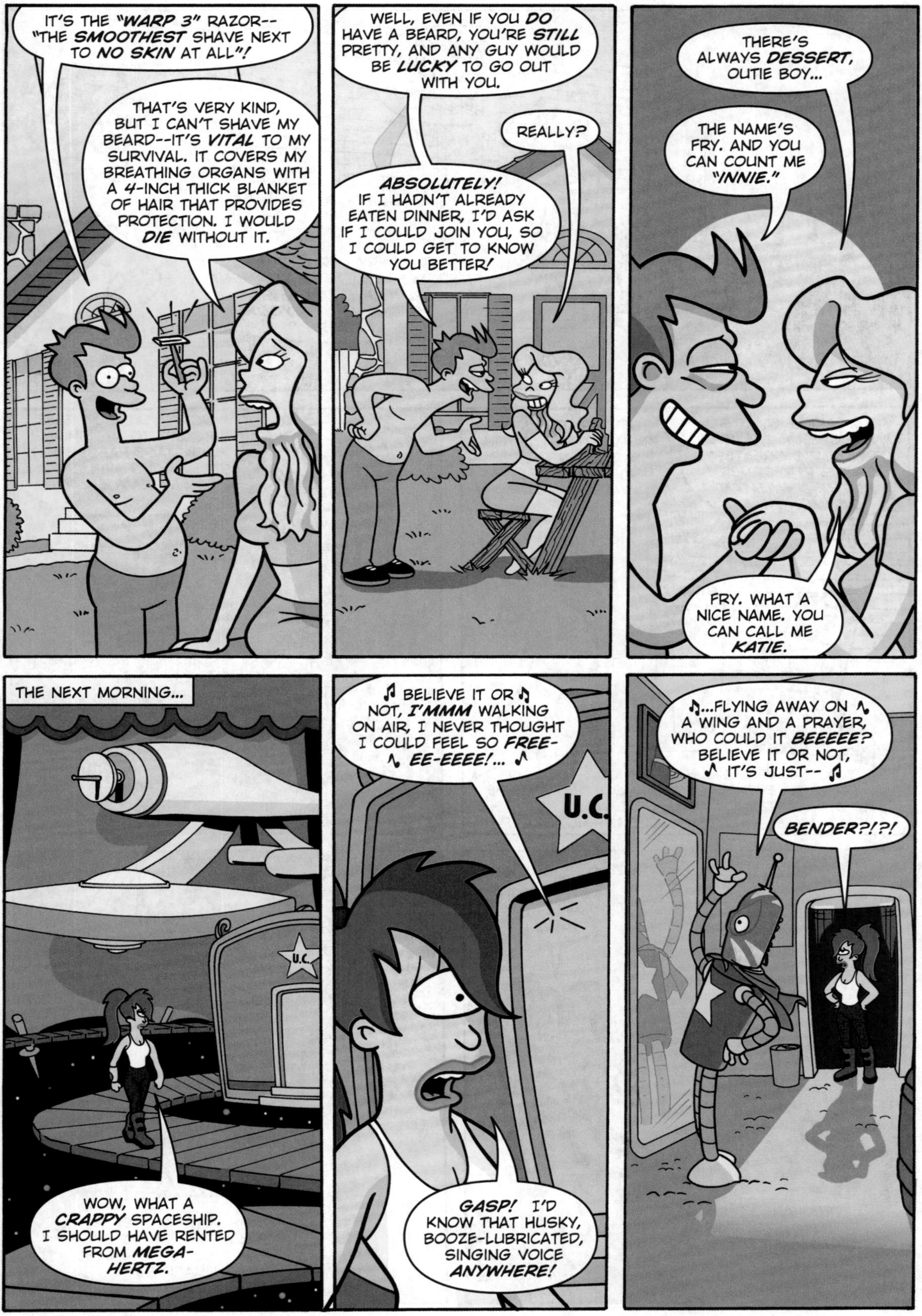
IT'S THE "WARP 3" RAZOR-- "THE SMOOTHEST SHAVE NEXT TO NO SKIN AT ALL"!
THAT'S VERY KIND, BUT I CAN'T SHAVE MY BEARD--IT'S VITAL TO MY SURVIVAL. IT COVERS MY BREATHING ORGANS WITH A 4-INCH THICK BLANKET OF HAIR THAT PROVIDES PROTECTION. I WOULD DIE WITHOUT IT.
WELL, EVEN IF YOU DO HAVE A BEARD, YOU'RE STILL PRETTY, AND ANY GUY WOULD BE LUCKY TO GO OUT WITH YOU.
REALLY?
ABSOLUTELY! IF I HADN'T ALREADY EATEN DINNER, I'D ASK IF I COULD JOIN YOU, SO I COULD GET TO KNOW YOU BETTER!
THERE'S ALWAYS DESSERT, OUTIE BOY...
THE NAME'S FRY. AND YOU CAN COUNT ME "INNIE."
FRY. WHAT A NICE NAME. YOU CAN CALL ME KATIE.
THE NEXT MORNING...
U.C.
WOW, WHAT A CRAPPY SPACESHIP. I SHOULD HAVE RENTED FROM MEGA-HERTZ.
♪ BELIEVE IT OR ♪ NOT, I'MMM WALKING ON AIR, I NEVER THOUGHT I COULD FEEL SO FREE- ♪ EE-EEEE!... ♪
U.C.
GASP! I'D KNOW THAT HUSKY, BOOZE-LUBRICATED, SINGING VOICE ANYWHERE!
♪...FLYING AWAY ON ♪ A WING AND A PRAYER, WHO COULD IT BEEEEE? BELIEVE IT OR NOT, ♪ IT'S JUST-- ♪
BENDER?!?!

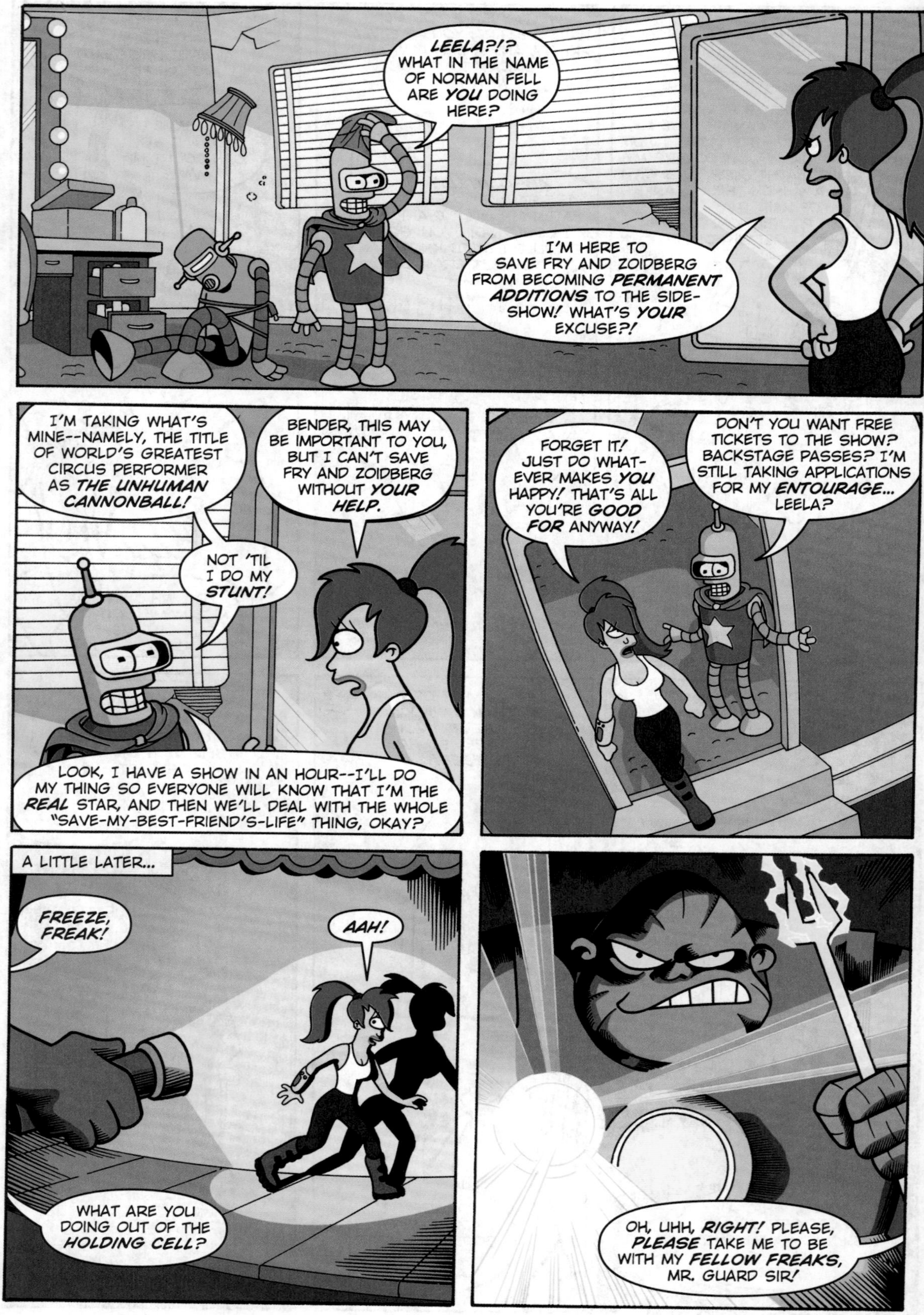
LEELA?!? WHAT IN THE NAME OF NORMAN FELL ARE YOU DOING HERE?
I'M HERE TO SAVE FRY AND ZOIDBERG FROM BECOMING PERMANENT ADDITIONS TO THE SIDE-SHOW! WHAT'S YOUR EXCUSE?!
I'M TAKING WHAT'S MINE--NAMELY, THE TITLE OF WORLD'S GREATEST CIRCUS PERFORMER AS THE UNHUMAN CANNONBALL!
BENDER, THIS MAY BE IMPORTANT TO YOU, BUT I CAN'T SAVE FRY AND ZOIDBERG WITHOUT YOUR HELP.
NOT 'TIL I DO MY STUNT!
LOOK, I HAVE A SHOW IN AN HOUR--I'LL DO MY THING SO EVERYONE WILL KNOW THAT I'M THE REAL STAR, AND THEN WE'LL DEAL WITH THE WHOLE "SAVE-MY-BEST-FRIEND'S-LIFE" THING, OKAY?
FORGET IT! JUST DO WHAT-EVER MAKES YOU HAPPY! THAT'S ALL YOU'RE GOOD FOR ANYWAY!
DON'T YOU WANT FREE TICKETS TO THE SHOW? BACKSTAGE PASSES? I'M STILL TAKING APPLICATIONS FOR MY ENTOURAGE... LEELA?
A LITTLE LATER...
FREEZE, FREAK!
AAH!
WHAT ARE YOU DOING OUT OF THE HOLDING CELL?
OH, UHH, RIGHT! PLEASE, PLEASE TAKE ME TO BE WITH MY FELLOW FREAKS, MR. GUARD SIR!

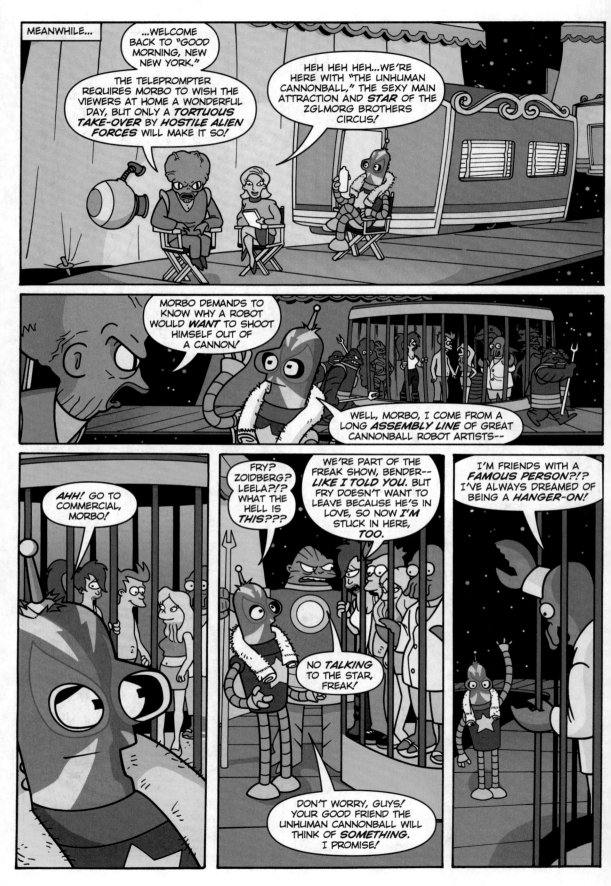

MEANWHILE...

...WELCOME BACK TO "GOOD MORNING, NEW NEW YORK."

THE TELEPROMPTER REQUIRES MORBO TO WISH THE VIEWERS AT HOME A WONDERFUL DAY, BUT ONLY A *TORTUOUS TAKE-OVER* BY *HOSTILE ALIEN FORCES* WILL MAKE IT SO!

HEH HEH HEH...WE'RE HERE WITH "THE UNHUMAN CANNONBALL," THE *SEXY MAIN ATTRACTION* AND *STAR* OF THE ZGLMORG BROTHERS CIRCUS!

MORBO DEMANDS TO KNOW WHY A ROBOT WOULD *WANT* TO SHOOT HIMSELF OUT OF A CANNON!

WELL, MORBO, I COME FROM A LONG *ASSEMBLY LINE* OF GREAT CANNONBALL ROBOT ARTISTS--

AHH! GO TO COMMERCIAL, MORBO!

FRY? ZOIDBERG? LEELA?!? WHAT THE HELL IS *THIS???*

WE'RE PART OF THE FREAK SHOW, BENDER-- *LIKE I TOLD YOU.* BUT FRY DOESN'T WANT TO LEAVE BECAUSE HE'S IN LOVE, SO NOW *I'M* STUCK IN HERE, *TOO.*

NO *TALKING* TO THE STAR, FREAK!

DON'T WORRY, GUYS! YOUR GOOD FRIEND THE UNHUMAN CANNONBALL WILL THINK OF *SOMETHING.* I PROMISE!

I'M FRIENDS WITH A *FAMOUS PERSON?!?* I'VE ALWAYS DREAMED OF BEING A *HANGER-ON!*

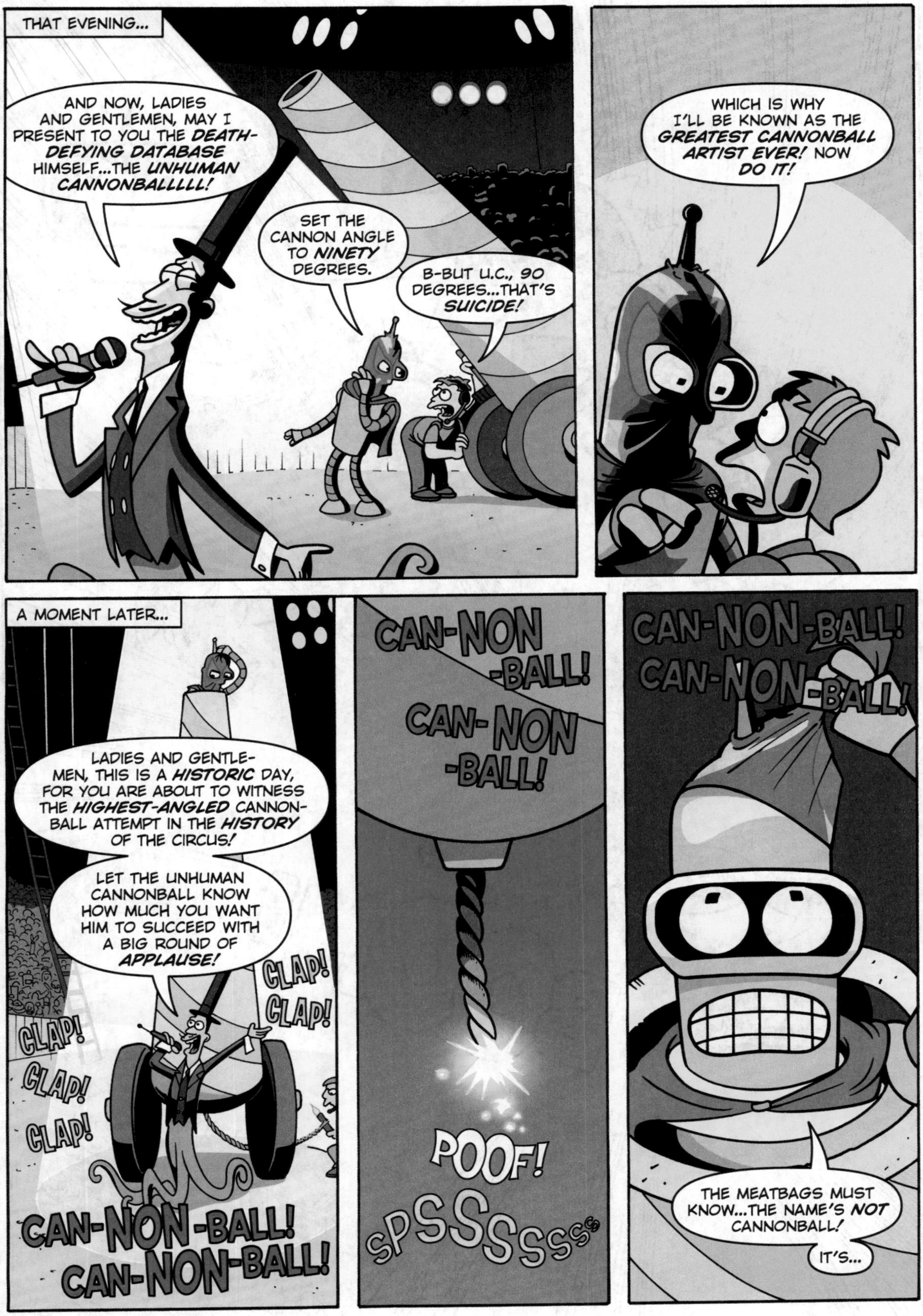
THAT EVENING...
AND NOW, LADIES AND GENTLEMEN, MAY I PRESENT TO YOU THE DEATH-DEFYING DATABASE HIMSELF...THE UNHUMAN CANNONBALLLLL!
SET THE CANNON ANGLE TO NINETY DEGREES.
B-BUT U.C., 90 DEGREES...THAT'S SUICIDE!
WHICH IS WHY I'LL BE KNOWN AS THE GREATEST CANNONBALL ARTIST EVER! NOW DO IT!
A MOMENT LATER...
LADIES AND GENTLE-MEN, THIS IS A HISTORIC DAY, FOR YOU ARE ABOUT TO WITNESS THE HIGHEST-ANGLED CANNON-BALL ATTEMPT IN THE HISTORY OF THE CIRCUS!
LET THE UNHUMAN CANNONBALL KNOW HOW MUCH YOU WANT HIM TO SUCCEED WITH A BIG ROUND OF APPLAUSE!
CLAP! CLAP!
CLAP! CLAP! CLAP!
CAN-NON-BALL! CAN-NON-BALL!
CAN-NON-BALL!
CAN-NON-BALL!
POOF!
sPSSSSsss
CAN-NON-BALL! CAN-NON-BALL!
THE MEATBAGS MUST KNOW...THE NAME'S NOT CANNONBALL!
IT'S...

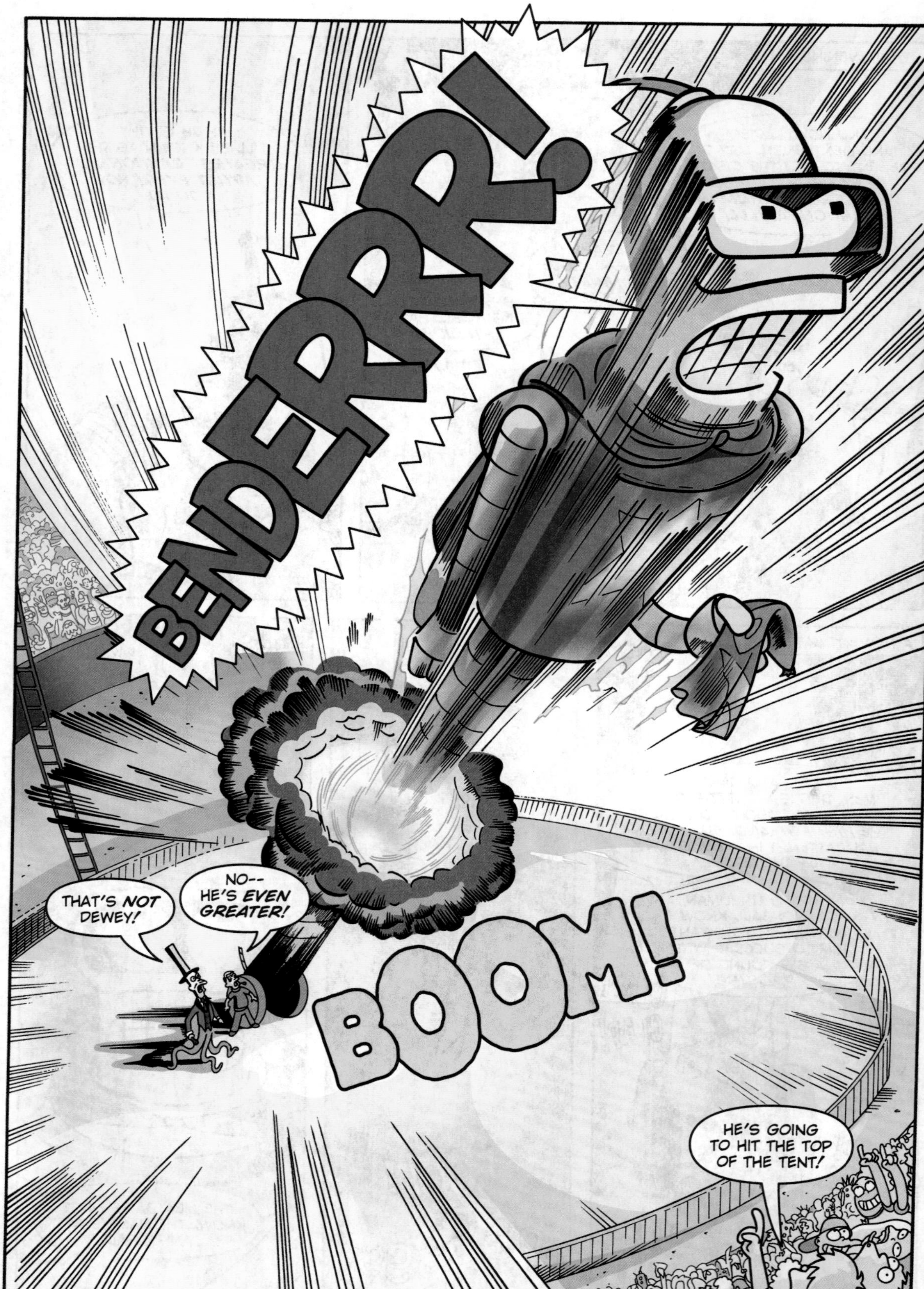
BENDERRR!
THAT'S *NOT* DEWEY!
NO-- HE'S *EVEN GREATER!*
BOOM!
HE'S GOING TO HIT THE TOP OF THE TENT!

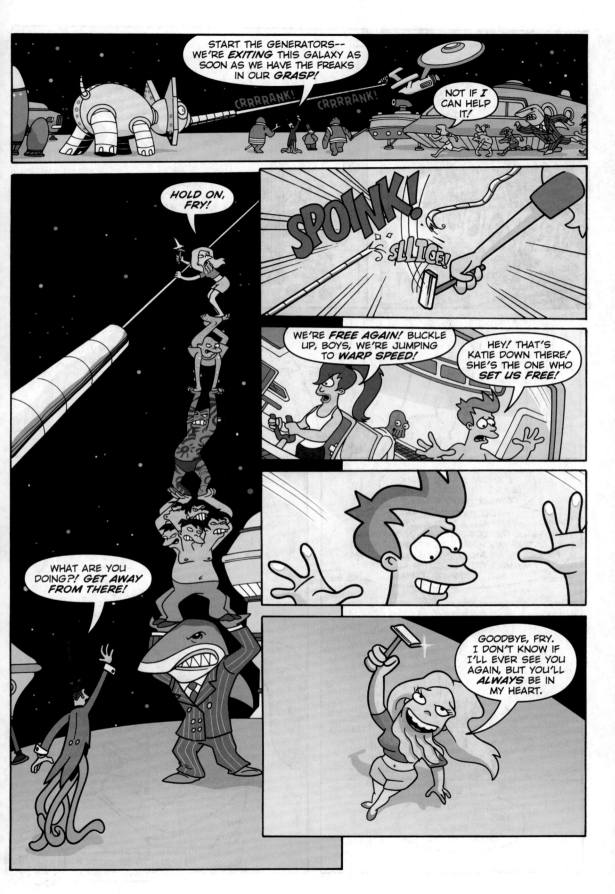

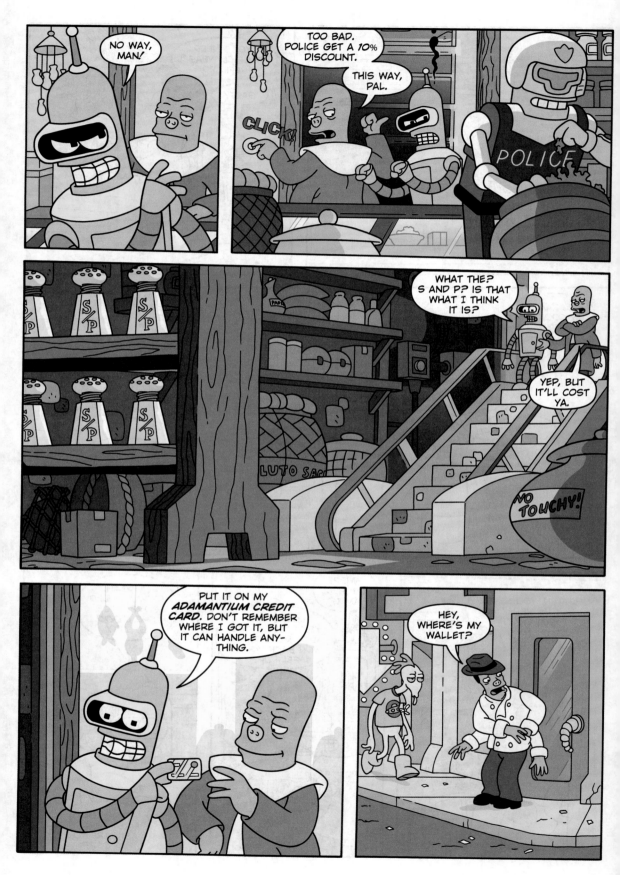

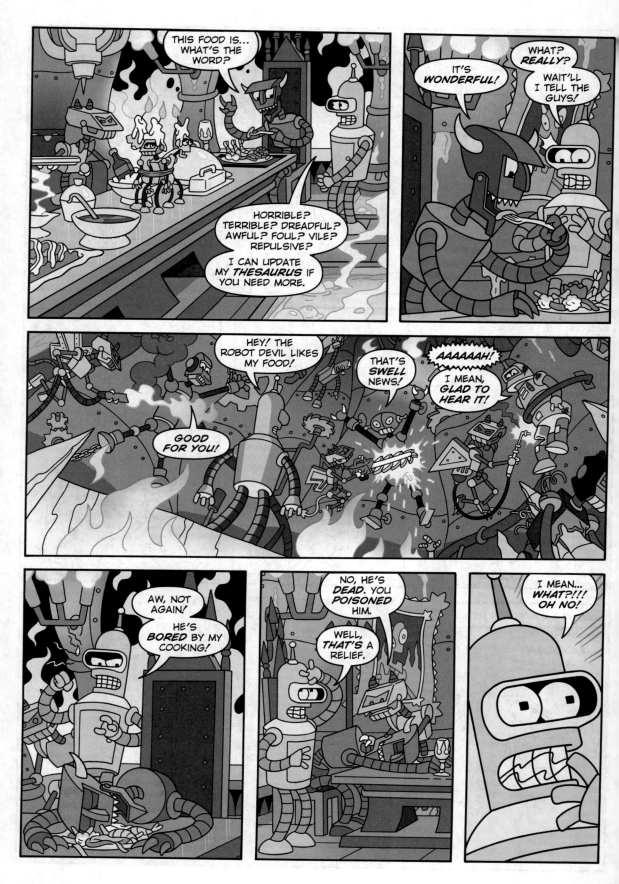

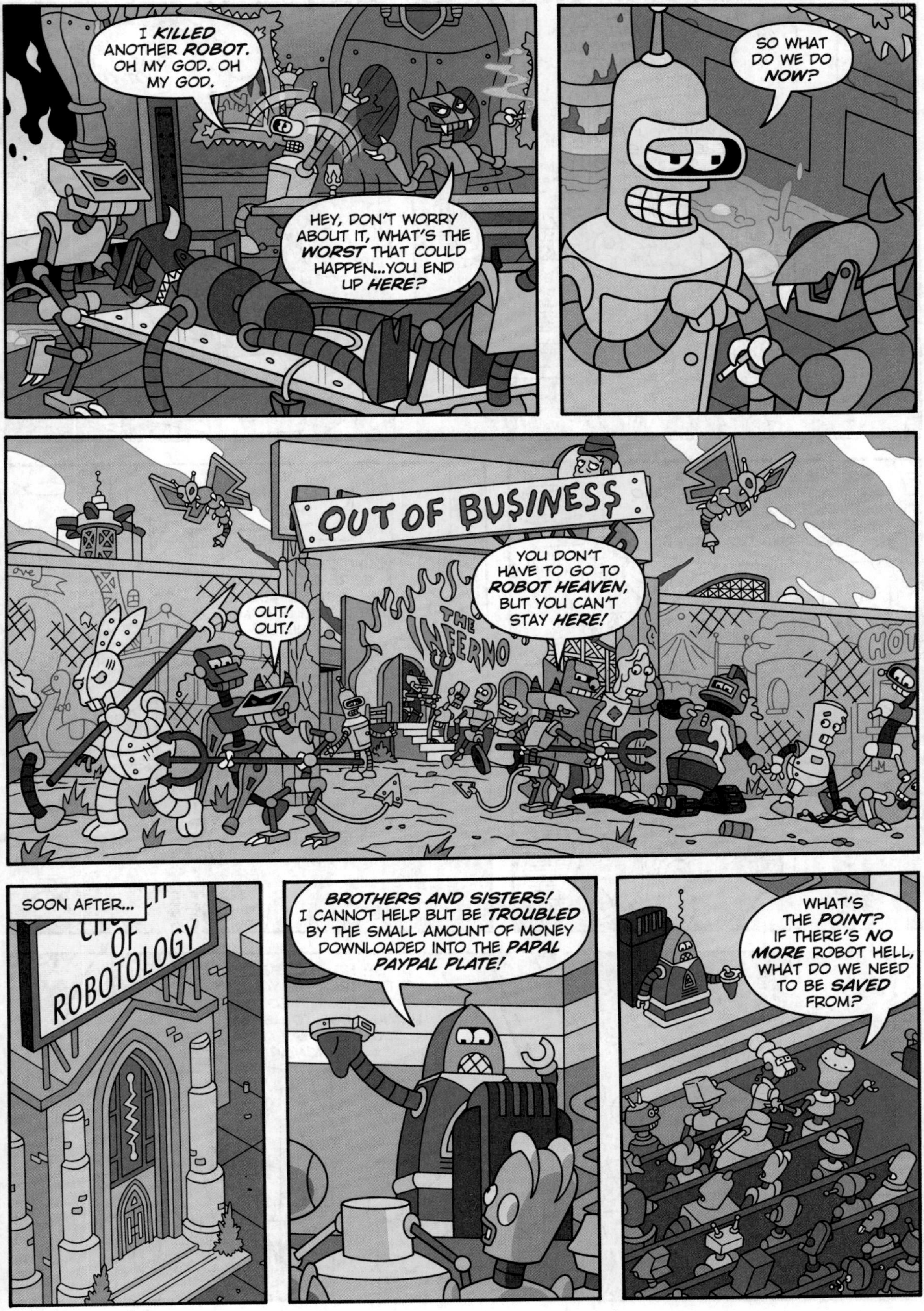

I **KILLED** ANOTHER **ROBOT**. OH MY GOD. OH MY GOD.
HEY, DON'T WORRY ABOUT IT, WHAT'S THE **WORST** THAT COULD HAPPEN...YOU END UP **HERE?**
SO WHAT DO WE DO **NOW?**
OUT OF BUSINESS
THE INFERNO
OUT! OUT!
YOU DON'T HAVE TO GO TO **ROBOT HEAVEN,** BUT YOU CAN'T STAY **HERE!**
SOON AFTER...
OF ROBOTOLOGY
BROTHERS AND SISTERS! I CANNOT HELP BUT BE **TROUBLED** BY THE SMALL AMOUNT OF MONEY DOWNLOADED INTO THE **PAPAL PAYPAL PLATE!**
WHAT'S THE **POINT?** IF THERE'S **NO MORE** ROBOT HELL, WHAT DO WE NEED TO BE **SAVED** FROM?

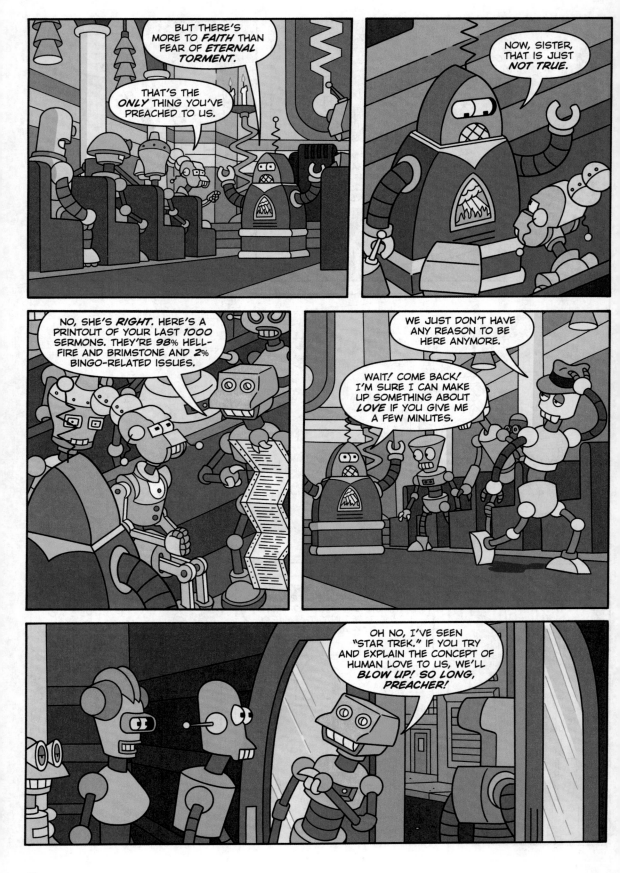

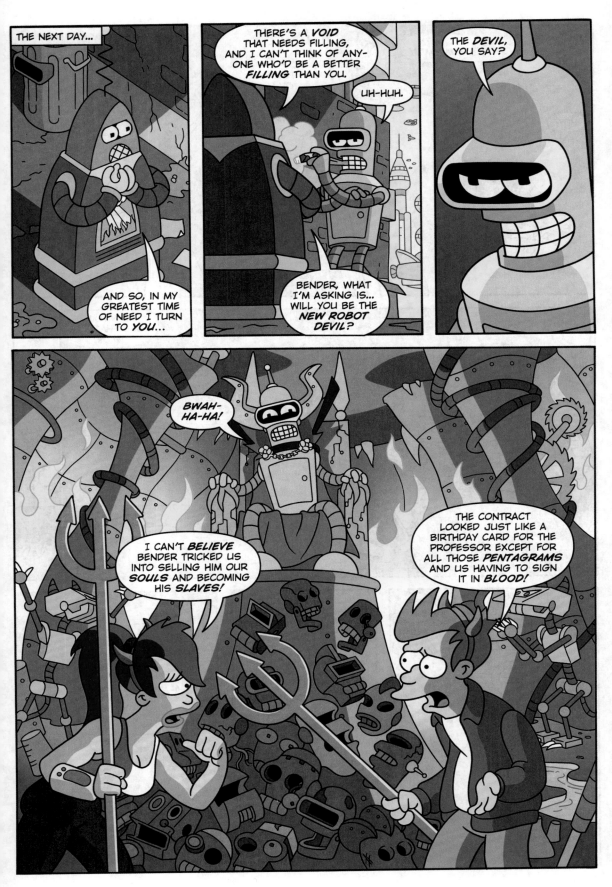

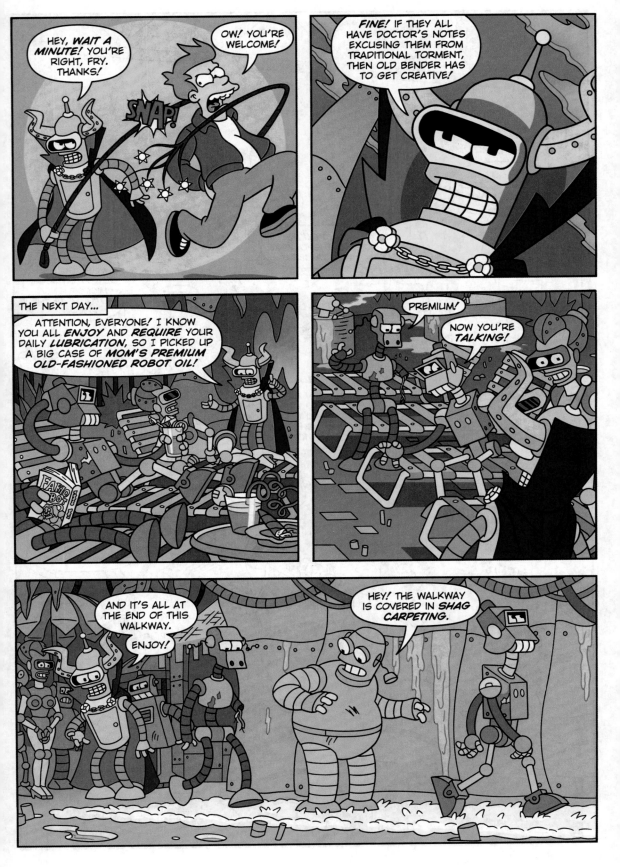

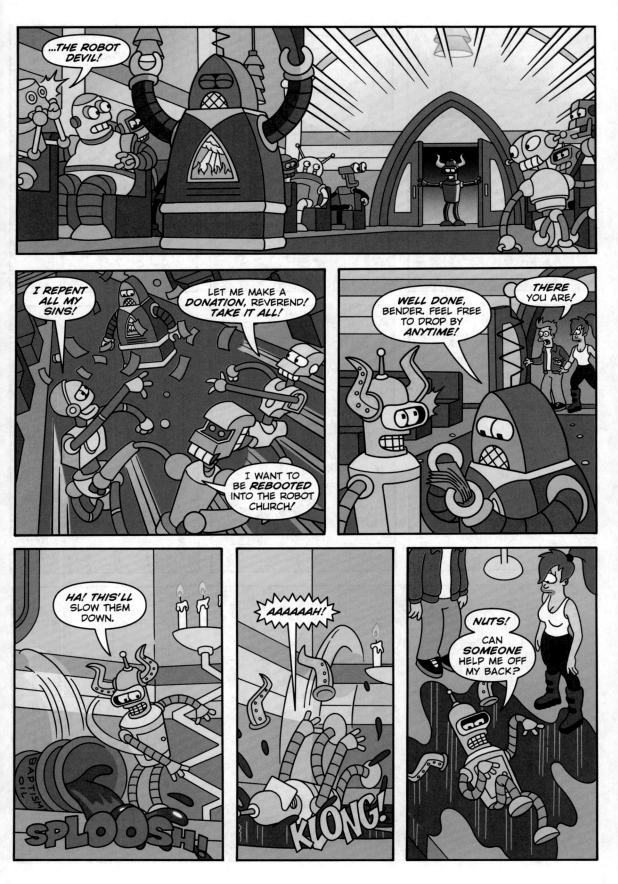

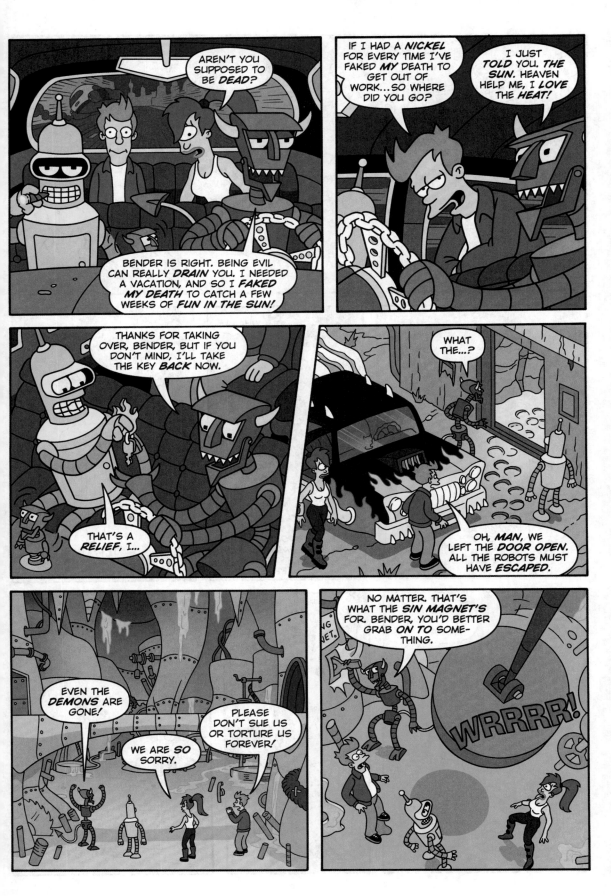

124

125

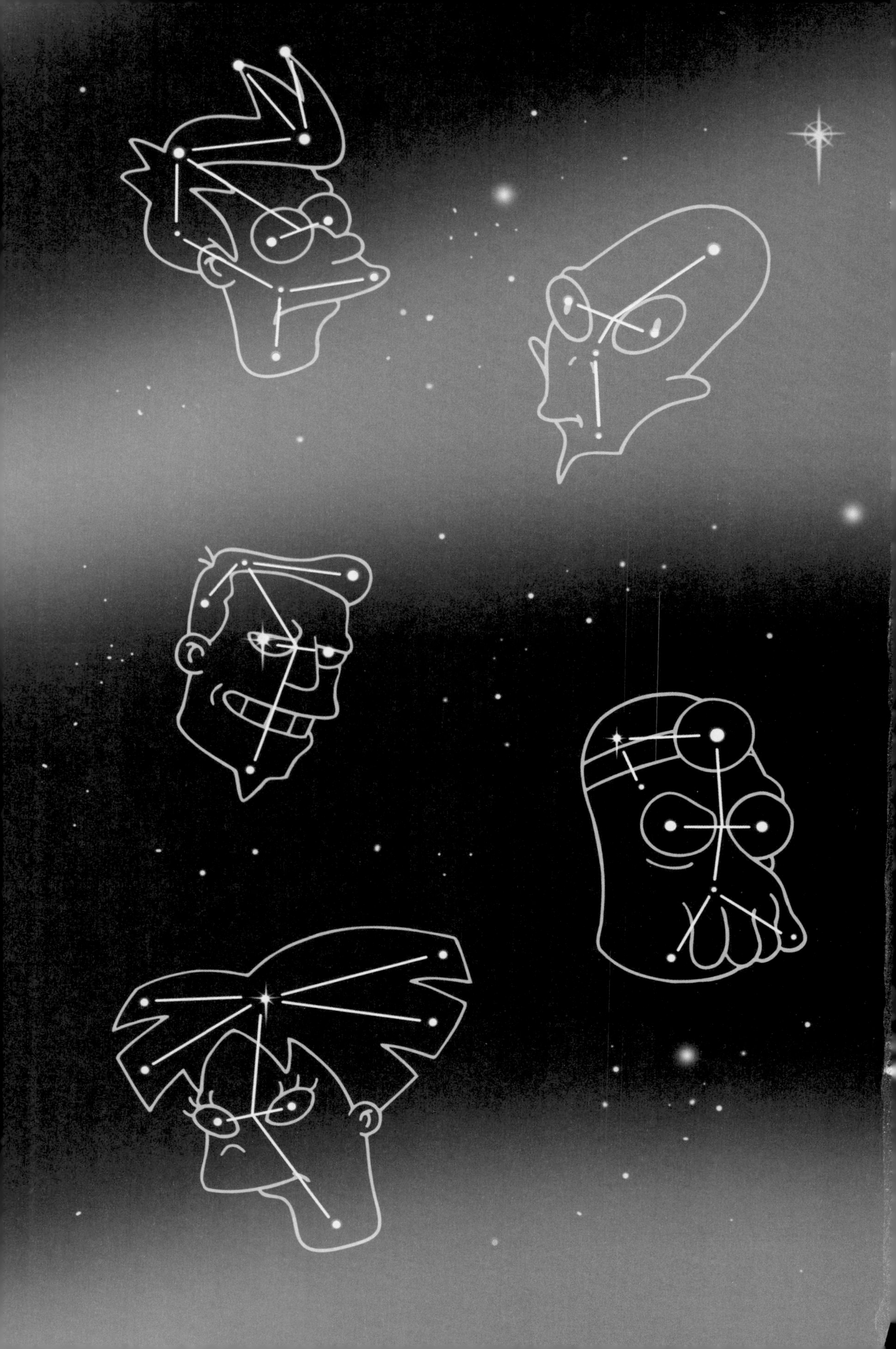